The Road Taken: A Memoir
One VW Bus, One Widow, Nine Kids

By

Therese P. Kramer

ISBN: 978-1-4251-1668-2

*We at Trafford believe that it is the responsibility of us all, as both individuals
and corporations, to make choices that are environmentally and socially sound.
You, in turn, are supporting this responsible conduct each time you purchase a
Trafford book, or make use of our publishing services. To find out how you are
helping, please visit www.trafford.com/responsiblepublishing.html*

*Our mission is to efficiently provide the world's finest, most comprehensive
book publishing service, enabling every author to experience success.
To find out how to publish your book, your way, and have it available
worldwide, visit us online at www.trafford.com/10510*

www.trafford.com

North America & international
toll-free: 1 888 232 4444 (USA & Canada)
phone: 250 383 6864 ♦ fax: 250 383 6804
email: info@trafford.com

The United Kingdom & Europe
phone: +44 (0)1865 722 113 ♦ local rate: 0845 230 9601
facsimile: +44 (0)1865 722 868 ♦ email: info.uk@trafford.com

10 9 8 7 6 5 4

Dedicated to THE SOURCE.
TPK

Edited by P. Damian Kramer and John E. Kramer.
Cover design by Robert B. Kramer and Don Wilson.
Illustrations by Mary T. Kramer.

The *Bergen Evening Record* ran this picture after I graduated from St. Thomas Aquinas College in Sparkill, N.Y., just weeks before our great European adventure. I am in the center surrounded by my children (clockwise from my immediate right): John, 3; Thérèse, 7; Mary, 13; Anne, 16; Edward, 11; Joseph, 14; Christine, 10; Peter, 4; and Elizabeth, 8. You may refer to this photograph to better know the cast of characters in this book.

Erma Bombeck

June 28, 1995

Dear Therese:

Do you know what your son John did? He
has such love for you that he wrote to tell me
about your book and the life that inspired it.
What a life it has been! I may have written
the book on Motherhood, but you have obviously
lived it. Earning a college degree while raising nine children alone is not a job for sissies.

I wish you well on your book and congratu-
late you on "mothering" a very nice man. John
loves you and so do I.

Kind regards,

Erma Bombeck

Author's Note

In the summer of 1968, newly widowed, I took my nine children to Europe. As you might well imagine, I've never been the same.

It seemed like a good idea at the time: celebrating my newly minted bachelor's degree with a tour of Europe, kids in tow.

How difficult could it be, I reasoned, riding around in the United States or driving through Ireland, England and a few European countries?

The Europe we navigated in a Volkswagen bus was rife with student unrest, but I hardly noticed, occupied as I was with sibling unrest taking place behind me courtesy of Anne, 16; Joseph, 14; Mary, 13; Edward, 11; Christine, 10; Elizabeth, 8; Thérèse, 7; Peter, 4; and John, 3.

In the months before we left on our trip, reactions to the news of our upcoming journey brought uniformly different reactions.

Women were aghast: "All that packing, all those kids, all that laundry to do while traveling. I wouldn't do it!"

Their husbands' eyes filled with admiration and wonder: "Great idea! You're a brave gal. Fabulous!"

Our trip was a similar mix of wonder and wonder-why-I-did-it.

This slim book is no substitute for Guide Michelin or Fodor's. It is just a look at nine kids, one bus, and one hopelessly optimistic and outnumbered widow.

Oxygen

The ride home that night from the pharmacy in Old Tappan was a lonely one, an oxygen tank my only passenger.

As I drove, I wondered about the circumstances that might prompt the tank's use. Knowing Bernard as well as I did, one thing was certain: The emergency would have to be dire before he would call for oxygen. Would it be another battle of wills similar to convincing him to see a doctor, his refusal adamant and my plea strictly soft sell? Or would I find him gasping for breath and hope to God that I could help him first and panic later?

I wept at the thought of my tall, strong young husband who would not live to see our children grown.

A soft rain had started. I turned on the windshield wipers and wished aloud that tears in the heart could be as easily dispatched.

I left the tank in the car, having decided that a quick retrieval from the garage the following day would be more easily accomplished with the older children in school. I needed time to get used to the idea as well.

Bernard regarded me and the tank with a less than welcoming look when I carried it into the house the next day. By now, I was able to offer a lightly tossed, "Look, you may never need this, but the doctor told us to have it in the house just in case."

"I won't use it. Take it back. I don't need it," Bernard protested.

"I know, but in case he should ask you if we'd picked it up … ," I started.

"I don't want it in the house. It'll frighten the kids," he said.

"It'll be fine," I answered. "You'll see. We'll simply tell them the truth."

"The truth? That their father is an invalid?" he asked.

"They already know that you're home because … ," I started to explain.

"Isn't it bad enough that I *am* home and not able to work? This is just going to make it worse. How do you think I feel? What are the boys going to think a father's role is?" he asked.

"I'll put this behind the white chair in the living room," I said as I walked past Bernard. "Who knows? You may not need it. It's there just in case. As far as the kids are concerned, they'll only take it as seriously as we do."

"Maybe you're right." He began to decompress now that the hideous tank was out of sight.

Thérèse came home from kindergarten as Peter and John awoke from morning naps. The five of us sat in the living room, the boys cuddled on our laps, slowly waking up as Thérèse related amusing kindergarten tales, delivered deadpan while we fought back laughter.

Her keen perception lent itself well to a flawless mimicry that overwhelmed her audience. Thérèse duplicated perfectly how one fellow student spoke; a boy with a lateral lisp she named "juicy Jack" who was in need of speech therapy. She also provided close imitations of walks and gestures of most students and the principal. She was an equal opportunity mimic. She presented a rogue's gallery of characters very seriously as so many annoyances overdue for correction. She pranced about the room and announced, "There's something behind the white chair." As the boys jumped down to check it out, Bernard winced in my direction.

"What is it?" she asked.

"It's a tank that has oxygen in it," I answered.

"Air has oxygen," Thérèse added.

"That's right, Thérèse. It does. How did you get so smart?" I asked as I sat her down next to me.

"We learn a lot of stuff in kindergarten," she answered. "Why is the tank here anyway?"

"Can we see the oxygen?" Peter asked.

"Show us, Mommy," John chimed in.

"It's for me," Bernard interrupted. He left it at that.

"Sometimes I tell you to take a really deep breath when you're cold and shivering. Then your body relaxes and you feel better," I started. "Well, oxygen will help Daddy take really deep breaths if he needs to. It's ah … Daddy's medicine."

Thérèse closed the discussion, "Now are we going to have lunch?"

"Great idea!" I said, thrilled to change the subject. "What does everybody want for lunch? How about cottage cheese and fruit?"

"Yuck!" Thérèse replied.

Before "yuck" grew to a chorus, I quickly offered an expanded menu. After lunch the children went outside to play as we watched from the wall of windows in the living room, Bernard with his coffee and I with my tea.

"Aren't we lucky to have them?"

His rhetorical question brought no argument from me. In just such a moment I expected him to ask me what life would be like without him. He never brought it up. Nor did I.

In retrospect, our unspoken agreement of silence on the subject was strange, yet I was a willing partner. What purpose would discussion have served? Bernard already carried the huge burden of serious illness. Dwelling on future events would have inflicted the additional weight of guilt for something over which he had no control. Better, we agreed — without words — to relish each day filled with the joy children bring and keep things as close to normal as possible. Most likely he thought that a discussion of his imminent death would produce tears of protestation. He wasn't much for tears. Better to leave quietly, peacefully, wordlessly.

And so it went.

Reality would swiftly convince me that at forty-one years old, I was a widow with nine children to raise alone. God willing, our lively crew — who ranged from two-and-a-half to fifteen — would grow and flourish.

I'm sure Bernard assumed that I would complete my last year of college and raise the crew that we had stormed the gates of heaven to have.

At times, usually in the midst of a severe thunder and lightning storm, he'd ask me to take him for a drive. Off we'd go and, usually because of the weather, seldom see another car. I often wondered whether atmospheric pressure caused great physical discomfort or if he had in desperation thought that an auto accident would take us both at the same time. Perhaps a friend to accompany him would have cushioned the lonely prospect of exiting earth at such a young age. Who knows?

The oxygen tank was called for only once, by me, as Bernard's lifeless body lay on the kitchen floor. A moment before, he had glanced from child to child around the dinner table, smiled and said, "I'm very proud of each one of you."

Their collective thanks came in the form of smiles. I stood up, began to clear the table and coaxed the laggards to finish up so I could serve dessert. Dinner and dessert that July evening were nothing to brag about. I had thrust my attention to a summer course in biology; two hours of lab in the morning, lecture in the afternoon, and evenings spent poring over text and notes. Science and math were never my strong suits: too many rules, much too organized, with no room for carefree right-brain possibilities. Nevertheless, I had reached the midway point of the course and the prospect of improved menus and free time for togetherness was right around the corner. Happy thought!

I said, "Finish up now. Ice cream for dessert."

The younger kids gasped and sang out, "Ice cream!"

I sat down. Bernard gasped just as the children had. I thought he was imitating their reaction. His left hand moved in slow motion along the tabletop toward me. His upper body leaned to the left ever so slowly. When his head reached table level I said, "Please Bernard, don't do this. It really upsets me," thinking he was once more crying wolf.

At times when I'd take coffee or a meal to him in our bedroom, he'd be hanging off the bed. It was his preview of coming attractions. How would I act or react when confronted with his actual death scene? These were far from happy occasions, breakfast tray dropped in panic one day, followed by a scream and a dash to his bed — all for a false alarm. "How *could* you?" I would demand. The balance of the day was spent in an icy chill.

Reality played more smoothly than dress rehearsals. Certain that this performance was one in a number, I remained totally cool … until his body hit the floor with a sickening thud. I thought this was going too far. There at my feet, he lay motionless.

I know how to end this act, I thought.

"Joseph, get the oxygen tank from the living room. It's behind the white chair," I calmly said.

When I told Joseph to bring the oxygen tank quickly, I *knew* Bernard would jump up and forbid it.

He didn't move.

Joseph took the younger children into the living room where he led them in gently whispered prayer. Still calm, I placed the mask on his face and ordered, "Take a deep breath."

No reaction.

"C'mon, honey. Just take a really deep breath, please. Just one!" I pleaded.

Nothing.

I pounded his chest, which was as hard and immovable as a brick wall.

Nothing.

His spiritless eyes stared, unseeing. I shut them. I prayed aloud and somewhere in the midst of the prayer, said, "Now maybe you'll know how much we love you."

Anne tried to revive her father. According to my beliefs, not his, I baptized him. Twice. Once, concentrating on the "matter and form" — applying water in the sign of the cross; the second time personalizing it with his name.

I knelt beside him and talked with him and wept until the children's prayerful voices drifting from the living room became my harness bell, as Robert Frost had written. Their sweet, sincere voices lifted in prayer reminded me that I, too, had "promises to keep, and miles to go before I sleep, and miles to go before I sleep."

I stood, walked through the dining room to the entrance of the living room and announced to the children, "Daddy is dead."

Six-year-old Thérèse was the first one to break the silence.

"Are you gonna get married again?"

"Thérèse, Daddy has just died," I nearly wept. "How can you ask me that?"

"Well, I loved Daddy and I want another daddy to bounce me on his knee," she replied deadpan, in loving tribute to her father.

"I know, sweetheart," I said as I joined the children on the sofa and sat her on my lap. "You loved Daddy very much and he loved you the same."

"So, are we gonna have to bury him?" she asked.

"Well of course we will," I answered her.

"We will?" she persisted.

"Yes," I repeated.

Chris, nearly nine, knew exactly what Thérèse was thinking. She reached over, patted Thérèse on the knee and consoled her sister with, "Don't worry about it, honey. We'll get a couple of men to do that."

I laughed out loud. How could I? My young husband's body was still on the kitchen floor, death, a new fact of life for us and I *laughed*. Thérèse was waiting for me to pass out shovels and march all to the backyard for a burial, Western-style, when she asked her question. She meant it literally: "Are *we* going to have to bury Daddy?"

It was the medical examiner's day off; a local doctor arrived in his place. Her communication in general had a distinct hesitant quality that I'd observed at several office visits with Edward as her patient. She placed her right hand to her mouth and uttered an audible "Hmmm," as if to prove she was in deep thought. Tonight was no different; she examined Bernard carefully, then looked at me. Her hand traveled to her mouth, "Your husband had … hmmm … trouble with his heart?" she asked.

"Yes," I answered, "unsuccessful heart surgery five years ago."

"Yes … well," she spoke through her fingers as she tentatively searched my eyes and her mind for just the right words or so it appeared.

I felt sorry for her in the temporary position she had assumed as medical examiner. I couldn't take the long pause, not tonight.

"Are you trying to tell me that my husband is dead?" I eased her into the uncomfortable role.

"I'm afraid … yes, he is," she offered.

"I already knew that," I said, and then added in an effort to lessen her burden, "It's all right."

Talk about role reversal!

She left and the mortician was called. He arrived soon after, too soon after, *much* too soon after. Bernard's dead body stretched out on the kitchen floor didn't strike me as strange. It meant he was still at home with us where he belonged.

When the mortician left with Bernard's body I was overwhelmed with grief. Now he was truly gone, out of our home and *physically* out of our lives forever. I couldn't stop the tears, the flood of tears. Mary, my sister, called the doctor for something to calm me. I insisted that I could stop crying on my own, but it was actually beyond my will to do so. I reluctantly took one tranquilizer: Tears eventually stopped. It did the trick. The remaining pills were placed on a top shelf out of reach for all but me, where they stayed until they were thrown out several years later.

I truly believe in facing whatever must be faced, even if it means having your heart torn to shreds. When that period has ended you arrive at the other side of the trauma stronger for the experience that you would never have chosen. Why postpone the inevitable with pills to dull the pain? I needed to stem the uncontrollable flow of tears. One pill had accomplished that. However altered our lives had become, I needed to live *my* life alert and alive without a chemical crutch.

How vividly I recall the snail's pace of time.

He died two hours ago.

Now it's four hours since he died.

Now it's 2:30 a.m., only seven hours since he was here.

My God, will the rest of life pass this slowly? What has happened to time?

I remember trying to write a description of my raw emotions immediately following Bernard's death. I focused on the value of an exact dissection of my feelings for future reference on the occasion of someone else's loss.

The thought of being able to empathize with another who was grieving was most important to me. I needed to be able to say, "I *truly* know what you're feeling. It is as though your heart or your spirit has gone to travel as far as possible with the one who has left, leaving an empty shell to go through the motions of living. The result is that you can't be where he is, yet neither are you here. You are suspended somewhere in between."

I don't know why the thought of helping some unnamed person deal with his or her grief at some future date was important to me in the midst of mine. I do know that empathy is a tender gift. A genuine acknowledgment of one's present agony and longing has a more authentic ring than hearing once more that "time heals all things," "you're still young," and that hollow favorite, "count your blessings."

It's kinder to get inside someone's grief and to tell it like it is. It is horrible. It hurts like hell and must be accomplished solo.

I turned our bedroom into an office/study. Nothing was the same, therefore nothing should appear the same, I reasoned. After several months I was no longer awakened, nauseous, in the middle of the night by the thud of his body hitting the floor with the haunting thought that I could have prevented it had I known he wasn't fooling.

Time, once again, traveled the fast lane.

Grief now came in unexpected waves riding an otherwise tranquil sea: fierce, all-encompassing, temporary.

I'd sit in class, learn something I couldn't wait to go home and share with him and — wham! — a fist in the stomach told me those days were gone. Forever.

Gut-wrenching has an indelicate ring, but no other words rival its accuracy.

Time passed, we all grew up together and for a while I was the tallest one.

The Yanks Are Coming

Bernard died in the summer of 1967.

The summer of 1968 has been etched on my brain as the "Summer of Infamy," but not for the obvious reasons. The spring had seen the assassinations of Martin Luther King Jr. and Bobby Kennedy; Vietnam was dividing the country.

But the "infamy" I recall was one of my own making: It started out with the idea of throwing a few things together and taking a ride through Europe with nine kids in tow.

"Keep it simple," I repeated over and over to myself. Thoreau had said it best in *Walden*: "Our life is frittered away by detail. ... Simplify. Simplify."

The simple preparations went something like this:

Anne, who was the oldest at sixteen, was given the job of ordering a Volkswagen bus — the only vehicle I knew of that would hold our crew — by telephone.

"Yes," she said. "I do have permission. My mother is right here, but has to stay off her feet due to a little mishap. If you tell me the exact amount, we'll send the check off this afternoon. Color?"

"Powder blue," I whispered.

"Powder blue," Anne repeated, and then holding her hand over the mouthpiece, said, "He's laughing and wants to know if there's another name for 'powder blue' since he's never heard of it. He also wants to know if this is a crank call."

"That's all right," I reassured her. "Maybe it's unusual to order a car by phone, but when he receives the certified check he'll know it's for real. Order the palest blue they have," I instructed.

"He says they're not making them in blue this year. Maroon, bright red or gold with a white roof," Anne announced.

I winced, "Yuck! What miserable colors. Forget red. Can't you hear the remarks about having our own fire company? Dark colors look dirty faster. Order the gold with a white roof and ask him to have it delivered to Shannon Airport early in the morning on June 26th. Oh yeah, we'll need a roof rack and a good radio."

"Yes, that's right," my efficient secretary concluded the conversation. "You'll have the check in two days. Thank you. Goodbye."

"Okay. That's great. Airline tickets and van all taken care of. I guess that's all we can do for now. Do you finally believe we're going to Europe?" I asked.

"I really do, but," she wondered, "will your leg be better by then?"

"It has to be," I declared. "That spill I took certainly has taken a lot of the shine out of moonlight on the Hudson."

"Very punny!" Anne observed, "I know you wanted to share one of your favorite things — the full moon rising over the Hudson River — but why did we get out of the car?"

"I wanted you all to hear the waves hitting the rocks — such a great sound. I didn't plan on hitting the rocks at the same time."

"Do you think this is some sort of warning that we shouldn't go to Europe?" Anne asked.

"Not at all. It's a test, an obstacle to overcome. It'll be fine, you'll see," I assured her.

"How can you be sure it's a test and if it is, what's the reason for it?" Anne wondered aloud.

"Well, the Lord knows that if life moves too smoothly I am apt to become bored, so He roughs things up now and then to keep me focused. Three weeks off my feet at this point is a beautiful bonus, not what I'd have planned in the midst of student teaching. Nevertheless a gift," I said.

"A gift? Three weeks in bed with your leg elevated is a gift? You have a strange way of looking at life," she said, shaking her head as she left the bedroom.

"Thanks for all your help, honey. Couldn't have done it without you!" I called.

13

"Mom, you're not taking us to Europe just to win a bet, are you?" Anne asked from the hall.

"Of course! I've never lost a bet in my life because I only bet on sure things. I'll graciously accept your five dollars as soon as we're airborne," I assured her.

"I can't believe this is really happening. I can't wait until June!" she squealed.

Alone in my room I echoed her enthusiasm and anticipated the "Second Invasion of Europe by the Yanks."

June arrived quickly with two upcoming graduations to celebrate, Joseph's from St. Anthony's Elementary School in Northvale, New Jersey, and mine from St. Thomas Aquinas College in Sparkill, New York. A summer-long party to celebrate our mutual milestones was the way I had introduced the trip to Joseph. It bombed. Neither he nor his younger brother, Edward, wanted any part of a silly trip to Europe, wasting the whole summer when they could have a really good time swimming and playing baseball.

Dale Carnegie's best suggestions fell on deaf ears with the two holdouts. Finally one day when I had returned from school, I found the following offering from the reluctant pair:

Dear Mom,

We don't wanna go to Europe.

We wanna stay home.

Who wants to see Paris?

Don't care about Rome.

Who wants to see Europe from a crowded old bus?

Seven kids are plenty. Forget about us!

We'd rather go swimming, play ball all day long.

Please Mom, don't make us — that's the end of our song."

Signed,

Your unhappy sons,

E.F.K. and J.B.K.

The Yanks Are Coming

The house was strangely quiet. Bright fellows, those two. Knowing my dislike of any excitement the minute I arrived home, they had left me not only the poem but time to digest it as well. I used the time wisely to outwit the enemy. I replied in kind:

Joseph and Edward:
Oh dearest handsome sons of mine,
I'm touched by poetic pleas.
Such ventures far from prose are fine,
My sentiments, though, are these:
Mother and father now I must be,
Certainly not by my choice.
I'd rather have stayed quite simply me,
Remember how soft was my voice?
Suddenly thrust into being the head,
When I relished so being the heart,
Promoted to leader is easily said,
I'm no more than playing a part.
And now you are making it *trés impossible*,
My darlings, my loves and my joys,
I'm finding it very hard to believe
That travel evokes all this noise.
I pray for help with downcast eyes,
Suddenly answers are flowing,
As Dad would have said, "We'll compromise:
You're going! You're Going! YOU'RE GOING!"
Signed,
Your inspired Leader,
T.P.K.

The big day finally arrived. The phone rang every five minutes. The girls busily read letters from strangers, which a newspaper article had evoked under the headline, "Mother of 9 Celebrates B.A. with Trip to Europe." Some writers wished us Godspeed, others asked us to keep a daily log in order to advise them upon our return of the best places to visit, eat, etc. These were filed under dreamers or jokers. The response our story had elicited amazed me.

Had I read about a widow preparing to take her nine kids to Europe, I might have been amused, but I wouldn't have written to the lunatic.

A card from an old flame caused a momentary stir among the natives, quickly squelched by Chris, ten, who ran around asking, "Do you think I'll get pinched in Italy? A friend of mine said that everyone gets pinched there. Think I'll get pinched?"

Friends of the older kids dropped in and soon a sing-a-long erupted around the piano in the living room. A quick survey of this scene convinced me that no help should be expected from the happy revelers. It did, however, afford me some relatively quiet time for packing. Six large suitcases were rapidly filled with stacks of clothes, some new, others newly laundered. Packing for ten for a nine-week jaunt took exactly one-half hour. The reason it took so long was that I was interrupted by two phone calls.

Upstairs, the sing-a-long continued. The group was reliving a recent production of "Oliver!"

"I'd do anything for you, dear, anything,
For you mean everything to me," drifted downstairs.

Not one to waste a good cue, I replied, "Will someone come and take these suitcases upstairs, please?"

Of course, they shouted back in unison: "Anything."

The sight of the luggage lined up at the garage door produced strong, peculiar feelings deep inside me. Butterflies were soon replaced by stark terror. "Why am I doing this?" I wondered. I cringe at being farther off the ground than a step stool would allow.

With the background music still going strong a few rooms away, I broke into a mental tune of my own: "Flying too high with some guy in the sky is my idea of nothing to do." A miserable voice within me, which was months late, asked: "Aren't you afraid of flying? How are you going to feel high above the clouds?"

"If we had parachutes it wouldn't be so bad," I thought aloud. "We could all jump when the plane is about to crash."

"Are you talking to yourself, Mom?" Ed asked, as he came in from the garage.

"I was thinking out loud," I answered.

"Did you say something about a parachute?" he asked.

"Pair of shoes," I mumbled. "I was mentally reviewing what I had packed."

"Mom, remember when we crossed that little bridge at Bear Mountain and you screamed 'cause I walked near the rail?" Ed moved in on the truth.

"Yes, I remember," I conceded.

"I asked Daddy why you were so upset going over such a little bridge and he said you were afraid of heights. Are you?" he asked.

"Well maybe a little," I lied.

"Would you feel better if you had a parachute, 'cause I could ask the pilot for one when we board the plane. Want me to?" he generously offered.

I wanted to shout, "Yes! Please do that!" and hug him for being sensitive, but I simply smiled, thanked him for his concern and told him everything would be fine. In the process, I halfway convinced myself.

Shortly after dinner my brothers, Jim and Joe Powers, arrived to drive us to the airport. We piled into two cars: the girls in white wool coats with green linen collars and cuffs. They were lovely and the picture they presented outweighed the sheer impracticality of dry cleanable coats for the trek we were about to begin. Washable windbreakers would have been a better choice.

Everyone was well prepared for the new role of unofficial American ambassadors. "Remember," I had cautioned them time and again, "We are Americans and are unofficially representing our country. Always behave in a courteous, friendly way. Europeans we meet will get a good impression of Americans."

"Are we getting paid for being whatever it was you said?" Liz, at age eight, wondered.

"No, honey, what I want you to understand is that we are Americans," I started.

"I already knew that," she shot back.

"All right. Think of it this way. We're all members of the Kramer Family and I hope that most of the time you all behave well so that I am proud of you. I expect you to use good manners and ... ," I tried to explain.

"We do that, Mommy," she said.

"I'm sure you do, but while we're traveling, someone may forget. People in various countries won't know us as the Kramers but as Americans. If we're rude, people we meet will have the impression that all Americans are rude. Understand?" I instructed. She did.

"Who gave us the job of being ambassadors and how come we're not getting paid when we have to be so good?" Ed asked.

A sibling admonished his brother that he shouldn't expect to be paid for being good, "'cause you're supposed to be good for nothing."

"Oh, London is a man's town,
There's power in the air,
And Paris is a woman's town,

18

With flowers in her hair," I said to no one in particular, remembering the Henry Van Dyke poem taught by a favorite teacher many years before.

"What does that mean anyway, Mommy?" Liz asked.

"I don't know exactly. Sounds like Paris is soft and gentle and flowery, whereas London is no-nonsense and military, but you know the best part, honey? We don't have to guess what the author meant. We'll actually see for ourselves. Won't that be wonderful? Aren't we lucky? We'll see where my Mommy and Daddy lived, at least the towns, if not the houses."

"Are we all set?" called Jim, carrying out the last piece of luggage to the garage.

"All set, Jim," I lied, the butterflies the size of buffalo in my stomach told a different story.

And Then There Was One

In those hours, days and weeks after Bernard's death, it was as though I had been dropped into a strange and desolate land: Widowhood.

Now there was one where two had been.

I was beyond numb, closer to frozen in time and space. I couldn't help myself at *this* moment in my life when I needed help desperately. I immediately thought of seeking professional help and was advised by a sweet, well-intentioned family member, "No one in our family has ever *done* that."

I interpreted that to mean that I was weak or at least acting weak and I'd better snap out of it.

Willing to give that opinion serious thought, I tried to *think* my way out of the dilemma. I spoke to myself attempting to act as my own sounding board.

"Okay, look around you. Most things haven't changed. You don't have to move from this lovely house. The children are strong and healthy. You're young and healthy, as well. So you're in charge now but you've always been in charge of the myriad tasks that fall to one whose title is "homemaker, student, maker and keeper of medical appointments, bookkeeper, landscaper, repairmen caller, chauffeur, counselor, coach/cheerleader." You simply need to continue to do those things you've done in the past. It's simple. Just keep on going. That's all."

I'd given myself excellent advice. "Keep on going."

That's what I *couldn't* do!

I was stuck, emotionally paralyzed.

I had thought I was prepared for Bernard's death with five years to ponder the inevitable. Many receive no warning; death is swift and unexpected. In their case I could understand shock, confusion and whatever this was that I was experiencing. But I'd had time to prepare, hadn't I? So, why wasn't I prepared? Why was I immobile? What had happened to the "can do" gal I thought I was? The "can do" gal was hit with the truth: CAN'T DO! Or more accurately, *don't* want *to do*! A good brain, time to prepare, the best logic in the world all amount to nothing when your "better half" has left the scene.

He had left and his leaving had left me powerless. I recall vividly thinking over and over again during this time, "This isn't fair. Twenty-four hours a day for five years I knew exactly where he was and what he was doing and now I don't know anything about him." I never entertained the notion of, "Why me?" The word "unfair" popped up exclusively when I dwelt on his *forever absence*.

Slowly I crept through August and September believing that I was on my way out of the woods. Then Bernard's death hit with hurricane force in October, our favorite month.

There's a melancholy to October, leaves abandon trees, night air holds a chill, shorter days, longer evenings with cold winter's approach announced by the full, orange harvest moon. Midway through the month was Bernard's birthday. The very things that had held such charm now descended upon me as so many weapons.

The long fall evenings we had enjoyed *together* quietly reading or studying now were simply long lonely hours that magnified my aloneness. *October had overwhelmed me.*

My brother, Joe, stopped by each evening and left when the children went to bed. I made no attempt at polite conversation; most evenings I couldn't.

On one of those long, fall evenings, Joe had left and the children were all tucked in. Hoping to chase the chill from the air and from my heart, I decided to start the first fire of the season. Returning from the garage with a few twigs for kindling, I opened the damper, held a match to the tightly wrapped newspapers then dropped the twigs on top. Taking this small action felt like a step in the right direction. I dropped into a sofa that faced the fireplace, ready to be warmed and soothed.

The fire started, as did a flood of tears as I remembered the day I "found" a smaller version of our marble fireplace while Bernard looked at bricks. We had chosen, loved and shared this view for nine years. The extraordinary fireplace as well as the entire house had been a most spectacular gift of love from him. I appreciated that. He enjoyed my acknowledgment. This was the first fire without him. It tore at my heart. Now what?

My sister, Mary, called from New Hampshire the next morning. Sisters are known for marathon phone conversations. This wasn't one of them.

"How are you, Therese?"

"Fine."

"Are you really?"

"Yes."

"You don't sound fine."

"I am."

"This doesn't even sound like you."

"It is."

"I'm coming down for a while to stay with you."

"You don't have to do that. I'm fine."

"If I needed your help, you'd be here in a minute, Therese."

"No, I wouldn't."

"Yes you would. I'm coming down. I'll be there this afternoon. I'll see you then," she hung up before I could protest.

She arrived later that crisp October day, convinced by my terse replies that all was not well. Days were filled with usual activities, school for the children and me, but evenings were distinctly different. Whereas days reflected a "business as usual" façade, evenings were filled with dialogues that led to monologues delivered by me. Mary listened and listened to more than three months of pent up thoughts and emotions I needed to share with an adult.

I'm not certain, but I think we had a glass of wine most evenings. Something had melted the foolish stiff-upper-lip attitude that had dictated self-sufficiency in all circumstances. I definitely needed a shoulder to lean on for a little while.

I have no recollection of the subject matter contained in the monologues. It may well have been the type of blather to which bartenders are subjected. One glass of wine was the catalyst that had freed my captive psyche. Mary nodded in agreement through many hours each evening. Had she hit the sauce in a big way, no one could have blamed her. Her therapeutic approach was definitely Rogerian: no advice, no questions, simply a sounding board with occasional nods and many "uh huh's."

When she left after ten evenings of the same, I felt purged, renewed, ready to get back into the game of life, with a put-me-in-Coach spirit. I was simply back to being me. Thank God and thanks to Mary, the R.N.-turned-therapist.

I had the urge to run to the nearest counselor immediately after Bernard's death for support and direction but was dissuaded from doing exactly what I *knew* I needed to do.

During the three months before Mary's visit, when I would hit an emotional low, there would often be a note in the mailbox from a kind, empathetic professor, Sister Ursula Joyce, O.P., offering perfect understanding for what I was feeling that day. It was uncanny.

One could credit her Ph.D. in psychology for the depth of understanding. I credit her loving, Irish heart, intense intelligence and the rare ability to place herself squarely in another's situation.

I well recall, as her student, the day she had been awarded her Ph.D.

Still an undergrad, filled with awe and admiration, I gushed congratulations.

"You must be so proud of your accomplishment," I continued. "All that hard work behind you and now you are Dr. Ursula Joyce. Aren't you thrilled?"

"Not really," she said, to my amazement. "What does it really mean? I just showed up and did the work. That's all."

This brilliant woman must have been aware at that time a mere Ph.D. was simply another cog in the vast wheel of her future accomplishments. When her biography is written, the title *must* be, *"I Just Showed Up and Did the Work."*

I shall be ever grateful for being part of her work in 1967.

Support groups I'm sure are effective for many people, but I'm not a joiner and couldn't bare my soul to total strangers. A close friend or two is a different story.

Healing comes in many ways. For me, the occasional understanding note from a friend and Mary's patient listening assured me that two people realized our plight and truly cared. It made me feel less alone in the isolated new world of: *and then there was one.*

Rough Crossing

"Kennedy Airport straight ahead," announced my brother, Joe. "Have you ever seen such a huge plane?" he laughed, knowing well the terror his question struck in my cowardly heart.

"Thanks a lot," I answered through clenched teeth.

"Yes, thanks a lot, Uncle Joe, for driving us to the airport," the girls echoed their thanks, differing from mine only in degree of sincerity.

25

Inside the airport, my brothers Joe and Jim Powers took care of the luggage then headed upstairs with the children.

I lagged behind, hoping it was all a bad dream and I'd wake up by the time I had reached the top of the stairs, stretch, yawn and greet the new day, secure in familiar surroundings, at home in Palisades.

I knew I was fully awake when a huge man with equipment slung over his shoulder passed me, taking three stairs at a time. He bumped me as he darted past. I called after him, "Excuse me!"

At the top of the stairs, Roger Bannister's only rival and I met again, this time face to face. I spotted him and his equipment and moved quickly to one side in order to avoid him.

It didn't work: Each step I took was mirrored by one of his. I finally asked him if he'd care to dance. He answered my question with one of his own. Thrusting a microphone in my direction, he asked, "Are you the woman who's taking all the kids to Europe?"

"No. Not *all* the kids," I quipped. "Just mine."

"Have you been on a plane this big prior to tonight?" he asked.

"I don't know. Show me the plane and I'll tell you."

This was no time for an airport confession, so I didn't mention the last and only other flight I'd endured was on a small prop plane from Bermuda to New York in 1949, during which, in exchange for a safe flight, I had made a solemn vow to: 1) NEVER fly again or 2) join a cloistered community — or both.

He didn't have to know this nor did the metropolitan area, which was privy to our little tête-à-tête via the airwaves. If the interview lasted longer I don't recall.

I was aware of hearing "Have a wonderful time," before I was fully prepared for what it meant — actually boarding the plane. Waving furiously in the direction of the terminal from the field gave me an extra thirty seconds. I was the last to board the Aer Lingus plane.

I have never discussed acrophobia with a fellow acrophobic, so I don't know if my attitude is "normal" for this abnormal fear of heights. Many have told me to have positive thoughts about flying. I do! I'm positive the damn thing is going to fall from the sky!

Freudians would have us believe that a fear of heights indicates a fear of a moral fall. Sorry, Sigmund, but a moral fall can be overcome with a contrite heart, forgiveness and a fresh new start. If the plane crashes, you're history!

As the cool leader walked down the aisle of the plane, it appeared that half the plane was saying, "Hi Mom. Isn't this fun?"

"Terrific! Wonderful! Really great, honey!" I lied as I walked the "last mile," and melted into an aisle seat.

Thérèse, who would be seven on the Fourth of July, was my traveling companion at the start of the flight. Ten minutes into it, she made a perfectly reasonable request: "Mommy, do you think the pilot would turn around and go back if I asked him very nicely?"

"I doubt it, honey. Why would you want him to do that?" I asked, thinking it was the best idea I'd ever heard.

"Well, I have this hangnail that hurts and I know it would be all better if I were home. It's the only thing that would make it better," she said, her big, beautiful golden-hazel eyes full of trust.

I wanted nothing more than to moan with her, but Mary, nearing thirteen, arrived on the scene. She announced to me and the rest of the plane, "Mommy, I was in the ladies' room and some dirty old man walked in. It was so embarrassing."

"Mary, please lower your voice and come here. I'm sorry. It's my fault for not telling you about the occupied button on the restroom door. You have to slide it to let others know someone's in there."

"Mommy," Chris, almost ten years old, asked, "Do you think I'll get pinched in Italy?"

"What would they pinch?" Mary demanded in a slightly louder voice than had been employed in the dirty-old-man announcement. The absence of an in-flight movie was hardly noticed, what with the show going on in the aisle.

"My hangnail is better, Mommy, but I really have to get home," Thérèse pleaded. "My friend is having a party and she'll be sad if I'm not there. Could you please ask the pilot to turn back? I'm sure he'd do it for you."

"Why don't you put your head on my lap and rest for a while, dear, and maybe by the time you wake up, we'll be in Ireland," I suggested.

This was another bluff. I couldn't possibly talk to the pilot: Too many people walking around could rock the plane. Thérèse joined the would-be pinchee across the aisle, stretched out and went to sleep.

No histrionics for the moment, so I closed my eyes and opened them only at the sound of John's sweet three-year-old voice inviting anyone lucky enough to have an aisle seat to, "Look lady! Look man! See the pwetty sun. The sun is hewe!"

"Mary, Chris, get a hold of John will you please?" I asked.

He was retrieved and planted firmly on my lap where he stayed while we watched the sun rise together. As we watched, we softly sang, "Moon River" and I forgot that I was flying. Such was the fascination of my dear little boy.

"Two dwifters, off to see the worwd. There's such a lot of worwd to see," he would sing.

As we neared the Emerald Isle, I relaxed a bit and there were many guesses as to whether the Volkswagen bus would be there on time and who would be the first to set foot on the Auld Sod. Then the most phenomenal thing occurred. I stood up, took two steps forward and slid into the seat next to a son of old Erin.

"Excuse me. I wonder if I could ask you a great favor," I started.

"Anything!" he replied.

"Could I possibly share the window with you? You see the reason we're starting our trip in Ireland is because I've heard so much about the forty shades of green and I'd love to see it from the air."

"Here, take the seat by the window. This is my eleventh trip back home," he said. "I hate to disappoint you but you'll see nothing of the forty shades till we touch down. As I say, I've been back ten times before this and I never once have seen anything different than what you're seeing right now: mist, always mist," he apologized.

"Well what could be better than Irish Mist?" I asked.

"A bottle of Jamieson's," he laughed.

"Tell me, are there really forty shades of green? The truth now, man. My father was John Powers of Drogheda and if you tell me the forty shades are blarney, I'll carry the secret with me to me grave," I coaxed.

He looked around rather suspiciously, then, to be sure he was not overheard, he cupped his hand around his mouth and said, "Forty shades of green? It's a bloody lie."

"Hmm, I had wondered about the possibility of *forty* shades," I nodded.

"No," he assured me. "It's not true. There's at *least* eighty!"

We laughed together like two old friends.

I wondered as I wiped away the tears of laughter from my face, why the life-sustaining gifts of *faith* and *laughter* are hardly mentioned in academia. Most likely because they can't be taken into the lab, weighed and measured. A true loss. In a few moments a stranger and I had shared a laugh and my height-induced paralysis was transformed into joy.

"I don't believe it!" he said, leaning toward the window. "The clouds are parting and there's a bit of green showing. I don't believe it. I think you'll get your wish after all. It's like a miracle. Look at her there in full view. Isn't she lovely? This happened just for you. There y'are, count the shades for yerself!"

Speechless while I drank in the *eighty* shades, give or take a few, which form the patchwork quilt of Erin, my new friend broke the silence.

"She's beautiful, isn't she? Too bad her biggest export is her children. I'd have given anything to stay. There was no work for me here but I run back every chance I get. Sad that, isn't it?" he said, choking back tears.

"It's pitiful that you're forced to leave when your heart is still here. It's exile, isn't it?" I observed.

"Right. You're right on the mark. That's what it is, exile with visiting privileges," he agreed.

"Will you being staying long this time?" I asked, drinking in the fact that in five short minutes two strangers had run the gamut of emotions.

"A few days at the most. I've come back this time for my kid brother's funeral," he said.

"Oh, I'm really sorry. All I was worried about was an aerial view of Ireland. I had no idea. I'm sorry."

"No need to apologize. You're not a mind reader, are you? I won't hear tell of an apology. I'm happy we met. I was sitting there wrapped up in me own thoughts and not the happiest ones at that. If you hadn't have asked to share the window, I'd have missed the whole show. I'll be ever grateful to you, daughter of John Powers of Drogheda," he smiled.

As he carried his heavy burden off the plane, Mary followed him closely and gloated, "First one to walk on Ireland."

Not to be outdone, Chris boasted, "First one to skip on Ireland!"

Next from Ed, "First to hop on Ireland."

Then from me: "First one to shout in Ireland: *Look for the bus!*"

We were met promptly by a gentleman who was there to show us to the bus Anne had ordered by phone. Actually, there were two people who welcomed us to the Emerald Isle: Ben, a man in his early fifties, and David, who appeared to be a boy of ten.

I looked at the adventure bus for the first time.

"There's certainly adequate room," I said. "Not crazy about the colors, light gold body with a white roof. Oh, well."

Ben opened the passenger door for me, the sliding door for the children. My job was to watch Ben drive the bus around the airport so that I could soon assume the role of chauffeur.

In no time, my order to pile into the bus was met by a chorus of kids, calling out where they'd sit:

"Front by the window!"

"Near Mommy!"

"Sliding door!"

"Way, way, way back!"

This call would become a mantra for the children for years to come.

In the age before mandatory car seats and seatbelts, John, at three, opted for a perch on top of the driver's seat, with legs dangling over my shoulders. He dubbed this, Captain John's seat.

From here, he shouted instructions, such as, "Don't hit that cow. It's a friend of mine."

THE ROAD TAKEN

After a ten-minute lesson on the art of driving the bus and driving on the left side of the roads, we left Shannon Airport and were on our way.

Death Moved In

Death moved in and for five years remained an unwelcome guest in our young, active household.

In June 1961, Bernard, at thirty-eight, had punctured his foot on a nail at a jobsite. He stopped at a local emergency room for a tetanus shot. Routine and simple? It was the beginning of the end of his young life.

I cringed when he told me the name of the hospital, but I assumed for such a simple procedure there was no cause for alarm.

My first reaction was valid.

That night he ran a fever, which alternated with chills and violent shaking. It was frightening to witness this unrelenting attack … of what? I still don't know for sure.

Thérèse, our seventh child, was due the next day. Her imminent birth had been paramount in my thoughts, particularly since we had almost lost her in the sixth month of pregnancy. I was grateful she had come to full term. There was a question of birth complications in the obstetrician's mind, but not in mine.

Early the following morning, concerned about Bernard, I called the doctor who made a house call. We lived in those days when doctors still provided such niceties.

His diagnosis was grippe, if I remember correctly. I picked up a prescription and made an appointment for an office visit two days later. But Bernard's chills and shaking wouldn't subside. I called the doctor again. On this house call, he ordered immediate hospitalization.

Bernard refused and I understood why; I tried to assure him that I'd be fine and could call on friends and neighbors for a ride to the hospital when Thérèse's debut was at hand. "Farming the kids out" among other stay-at-home moms was an option in those wonderfully normal days when mothers were mothers, not bread-winners. He would not hear of it.

Thérèse appeared about ten days late and came booming into the world, hale and hearty on the Fourth of July, 1961 — thank God, with no complications. I was grateful for the ten days I had at home with Bernard before she was born. It gave us time for much-needed TLC since he had opted against a hospital stay. He not only drove me to the hospital on the morning of the Fourth accompanied by the six kids, he insisted on visiting each evening for full visiting hours. He shouldn't have. He was much too weak.

On July 7, when we brought Thérèse home to all her welcoming siblings, we followed the usual routine. Each child, seated on the couch with the help of a pair of supporting hands, kissed and welcomed our newest gift from God. I would then hold the baby and ask the group, "Do you love her?"

"Oh, yes!" they assured me.

"Should we keep her?" I asked the group.

"Oh, yes!" they all insisted.

Of course, I later used this against them when they would complain about one of their younger siblings: "Look, I gave you a choice the day I brought her home from the hospital." Or, "You were the ones who wanted to keep him!"

With Thérèse fed and settled into her new home, I immediately packed a bag for Bernard and drove him to Pascack Valley Hospital two weeks after he had been ordered to check in. I was, of course, dressed in some "smart maternity number," having delivered four days prior to his admission.

Enter comic relief! The reaction of the receptionist when I entered carrying Bernard's overnight bag was immediate and priceless albeit unflattering. She took one look at me, called maternity to get there — "stat" — and literally shoved me into a wheelchair. I laughed, stood up and informed her that I had already "done that." The patient was my husband, who preferred a room in the medical wing (rather than the maternity wing) if possible.

Not that we were finished with maternity floors: Two additional trips to Holy Name Hospital swelled our ranks to nine children.

Once doctors saw him, he was admitted for a week or two — poked, prodded and tested. Then came a string of office visits.

A local M.D. had recommended Bernard see another doctor for a cardiac workup, which should have resulted in a precise diagnosis of his heart's condition. What stands out still as this second doctor's main fascination was mechanical rather than human: He discovered that Bernard's heart made five distinct sounds.

I was not present for the appointment. I questioned what the many sounds had to do with an accurate diagnosis. The patient didn't know, but reported that the doctor was interested in recording the individual sounds. A short time after this meeting with "the sound man," Bernard had an appointment with a doctor at Columbia Presbyterian Medical Center in Manhattan. I was to accompany him.

I had spoken with several people who had undergone cardiac surgery, in an effort to prepare. Mostly, I planned to listen to what the expert proposed and ask when he would perform the heart catheterization, which, I had learned, was apparently standard procedure prior to surgery.

The day for our appointment arrived. With plenty of time to spare, I had only to drop the little ones at my sister's house a few miles away then accompany Bernard into the city. At the last minute, he changed everything, saying he was a big boy and could handle this appointment by himself. Off he went.

I was devastated, canceled babysitting plans, changed clothes and tried to be involved with business as usual at home. With my little ones at home, there was always plenty to occupy my attention and interest.

But my mood was less than serene. I was aggravated and resentful to have been excluded from this important meeting. "Henceforth you belong entirely to each other." I cherished each word of our wedding vows and that day knew the heart, which happened to live in his body, belonged to me, as well. Didn't he know that? Why was he treating me like this? There could never be an acceptable explanation. None was offered.

Bernard was a classic strong-silent type.

Had growing up without a father left him unschooled in how to communicate within marriage? Had his refusal to include me in the all-important interview been his attempt to protect me in case the prospect of recovery wasn't good? I'll never know. Throughout or marriage, I gave him the benefit of the doubt, adjusting my expectations regarding his behavior when necessary. This was one of those times.

I was certain there were a million things he didn't understand about me, but there was one major difference: I had the ability and desire to be understood. If he had a question about anything I'd said or done, I'd try my best to explain. In this area, there was no reciprocity.

When the domestic atmosphere had defrosted slightly, Bernard announced that he was scheduled for a simple operation as heart surgeries go, to open the mitral valve that was stuck shut — mitral stenosis.

"Did he discuss cardiac catheterization?"

"No."

"I understand this is standard procedure."

"I don't know. The doctor didn't mention it. He'll probably do it when I'm in the hospital."

"How many of these procedures has he done?"

"I don't know."

"This is nothing to fool around with. Why don't we go to the best in the country? Why not a second and third opinion?"

"It's all set up. It'll be fine. It's scheduled for February twenty-eighth."

"I know I've had the best doctors. It's great to have that security. Won't you please consider another opinion or two from the best men in the field? I'll fly anywhere with you to consult with the best. Please think about it."

"It's all set up."

"Who cares? Schedules can be changed, surgeries canceled or postponed."

For Bernard, the first opinion would be the only opinion. No time to waste.

On the day of the surgery, I arrived at the hospital much too early. Waiting in a solarium, a woman asked if I was waiting for someone to come from surgery. I told her I was waiting for my husband but realized I had jumped the gun and most likely had a good wait ahead of me. She asked the nature of the surgery and the name of the doctor. I explained in layman's terms.

When she heard the surgeon's name, she asked, "Oh, is he performing heart surgery now?"

I felt instantly nauseous.

I think I left to do something about the car, which I'd left parked on the street. When I returned, the surgeon met me at the elevator.

"Mrs. Kramer?"

"Yes."

"I'm Dr. MacAllister. Let's go into your husband's room for a moment."

As we walked the short distance, I asked, "Tell me. How is he? How did it go?"

"He came through surgery very well."

"Thank God. Now I think I'll check in for a couple of weeks to recuperate from this whole thing."

Assured that he had come through it very well foretold a happy ending, didn't it? That rosy prospect changed as we crossed the threshold of his room, where reality struck loud, clear and to the essence of my being, with the doctor's words: "I should never have touched him. I wish this morning I were a farmer, a truck driver, anything but a doctor to have to tell you this," he said, looking at a picture of our seven children on the hospital dresser.

"Poor Bernard," I cried. "He was so hopeful when he told me not to worry last night. What went wrong?"

"It wasn't what we had thought. Our diagnosis was wrong. I shouldn't have touched him," he repeated as he shook his head and looked at the floor.

"Dear God, all this for nothing," was the only thing I could say.

"He won't be back in his room for several hours. I think you should go home and come back later," he said as we walked out of the bedless room.

I don't recall the elevator ride, the walk to the car or the ride across the George Washington Bridge at all. The only part of the lonely solo trip that I remember was a scream of disbelief that started at the beginning of the Palisades Interstate Parkway in Fort Lee, New Jersey. Where it stopped or if it stopped on the twelve-mile ride to Palisades, New York, I don't know.

Unexpectedly, Jim George, a neighbor, was waiting at the door when I drove up to the house. I was unaware that anyone on the street knew about Bernard's surgery. We all lived rather privately. I was at once shocked and pleased to see him there.

"Well, how'd it go?" he asked. "Is he going to be OK?"

My answer to a man I hardly knew was a torrent of tears. I heard myself say, "He is my life!"

Jim offered something in the way of consolation concerning a serious illness his wife had survived some years before. He told me that he knew how I felt. That was comforting. Until then I had felt alone in a violent storm, tossed, battered, with drowning a distinct possibility.

During his three-week hospitalization, I spent every day with Bernard, thanks in no small part to friends and relatives who divided up the kids, all of whom chose that exact time to come down with the chicken pox. Remarkably, all the stand-in moms still talk to me.

Bernard suffered a great deal during his hospital stay, from stubs of ribs, which had been sawed from the back, a procedure that seemed archaic at the time. The incision started at the breastbone, traveling a horseshoe path to mid-back.

Soothing his suffering as much as possible was easy in comparison to acting relieved and happy with him when he had yet to be told the sorry news. After the doctor finally explained the whole thing to him, he said he already knew the prognosis wasn't good by looking at my face. No poker player, I.

At home and comfortable, he relaxed with all the children showering him with love and care. Soon enough, there would be two more children to offer love and receive it.

In the eyes of the world I was insane for having more children.

"Your husband is dying," I was often reminded. "He has very few years left to live and you're having another child or two? Why?"

"Why not? If I can raise seven, why not nine?"

Peter, due in January 1964, arrived early in December 1963, three weeks after President Kennedy was slain. Our new son was a wonderful way to brighten those dark days and guarantee us a happy Christmas.

His Daddy finally had the joy of watching, from day one, the development of one of his children. With the other children, he had only seen them for a while in the evening since his workdays were long. What a match: Peter and Bernard were inseparable.

When I was pregnant with John, who was born January 13, 1965, a woman whom neither of us knew stopped us as we entered a school function. She tapped me on the arm and announced, "You're pregnant!"

I had a nasty urge to observe my condition and exclaim, "You're right! By gosh, I am!" but I resisted. Instead I smiled and acknowledged the fact. She was not pleased with such a passive response, happy though it was.

She continued, "But don't you remember? Your husband was very ill? We prayed for him in church?" I assured her that I certainly remembered and thanked her for her prayers. Still not happy, she said, "But you're *pregnant*! And your husband was so ill!"

I looked her square in the eye and said, "It was his *heart!*"

Having two children who certainly would have no memory of a father was an act of madness to some people. To others, it was an act of courage. It was neither. Peter and John are gifts of limitless joy who have enriched our lives abundantly. As one interested in accumulating wealth continues to increase his holdings, my treasure in the privilege of motherhood was multiplied nine times over. *How wonderfully blessed I have been.*

Erin

After a ten-minute lesson on the art of driving the VW bus and staying on the left side of the road, we left Shannon Airport and were off.

The first children we met in Ireland were tinkers' children —
beggars' children — outside a restaurant in Limerick. We came
out after a hearty meal, with smiling faces and full tummies.

"Please Mum, moony. Please Mum. Moony for food," they
pleaded.

"Why don't you take them into the restaurant and buy them
dinner?" Ed asked.

"No, no," they interrupted. "Moony Mum for food."

"You're hungry?" I asked, confused at their refusal of a hot
meal.

"Oh yes, Mum. Very hungry," they insisted.

"Well, if you don't want to eat in the restaurant, let me buy
you some milk and bread and whatever else you want. Fruit, meat,
whatever," I offered.

"No Mum. Me Mum would kill us if we took food. Moony
please, Mum," they insisted.

"Poor little kids," Chris said. "Couldn't we take them to our
bed-and-breakfast and clean them up?"

As I reached for my wallet still wondering why hungry children had refused the offer of food, a woman interrupted my reach.
She said these were tinkers' children and as such were sent out to
beg for money that parents would squander on whiskey.

"But they look so needy and most likely *are* hungry, don't you
think?" I asked.

"They refused the meal you offered, didn't they? I'm telling
you to put the money away, unless you want to *throw* it away," she
advised.

Walking away, with my well-fed crew — and the tinkers' kids'
"please Mum" still ringing in my ears — was not easily done.

A pensive mood settled on the children that evening and there
were many comments about the tinkers' children. I understood
their dilemma — a feeling of helplessness — not willing to sup-

port or contribute to the habit of the parents but at the same time unable to help the children. Every once in awhile, someone would ask, "Why don't they wash their children's faces and hands at least?"

The remark that warmed my heart was, "Good thing you don't drink, Mom."

"Well, the trip isn't over yet," I reassured them.

"You mean we could be out there begging on the street to pay for your whiskey?" Ed asked.

"Relax. Should I hit the bottle, I'll pay for my own," I laughed. But apparently Ed's question was serious; I heard a loud "phew" from the back of the van.

Soon we were off to Cork and settled in at the Imperial Hotel, where we had breakfast and dinner daily, lunch unplanned was on whichever road we happened to find ourselves. Our stay in Cork was fun. Mary became fast friends with Henry Finn, one of the waiters. This friendship came with fringe benefits: multiple desserts after dinner and, on one occasion, a separate table for Mary where Henry joined her for dessert.

Speaking of Mary. …

One evening as I dashed around my room prior to joining the crew in the dining room, I had only to slip on my dress when Mary burst into the room with a soccer team from Spain, which was in Cork to play their Irish counterparts.

"Mary! I'm in my slip!" I announced.

"I know. It's pretty. I didn't know you wore black. …" she started.

"Mary, I'm not dressed! What are you *doing*?" I asked as I reached for a robe.

"I'm going to a soccer game and a party with the Spanish team. They invited me. I told them you speak Spanish, so they wanted to meet you. This is my mother," Mary announced.

"Bonjour!" I smiled.

"Mommy! That's French!" Mary observed.

"I know it's French! I think better with clothes on!" I responded.

Partially covered and recovered, I turned to Mary and informed her, "At the moment, the only Spanish I recall is, let's see, parts of several dialogues: 'I prefer pure air and blue skies.' Oh yeah, and 'I was going the wrong way on a one-way street.' And the really appropriate one that demands, 'Mama, come here. Look how I can walk on my hands.' Now from that vast repertoire, which would you like me to deliver to the entire Spanish soccer team that I met while half-naked in the middle of Ireland?"

"I'm sorry but they have to leave now, I wanted to get your permission. I don't feel hungry. I'll skip dinner," Mary went on.

"Don't be ridiculous!" and "Not on your life!" must have a universal ring when delivered by an irate mother of a thirteen-year-old girl. The entire team sort of slunk away with an ever-so-soft "adios," the lone reminder of their presence, lingering in the hall.

When Mary and I entered the dining room together, I apologized for being late and asked four-year-old Peter why he sat with his hands on his lap.

"Peter, why aren't you eating?"

He looked up as I sat next to him and said, "How can I eat? I have no fish knife?"

The Brits called us Yanks. At that moment, Peter inspired an adjective as he sat, shoulders squared, waiting for the proper knife; he was indeed a Regal Yank. Even then Peter, now a journalist, was a wordsmith: every evening he would order Chantilly Trifle for dessert. Out of a selection of fifteen possibilities, his consistency was remarkable, "Chantilly Trifle, please."

What was even more remarkable was his apparent disbelief when dessert was served. The waiter, a most patient older gentleman, and I had a nodding agreement, which we both took very seriously. I didn't order dessert, so each evening when Peter protested vehemently that he had ordered ice cream, the waiter would wink at me, smile and place the trifle at my place, offering Peter the ice cream that he "happened" to have on the cart. Our assumption was that Peter loved the way it sounded. Ice cream has such an ordinary ring but Chantilly Trifle, ah now there's beauty in the very way the words slide from the tongue. I filed this experience with the lack-of-a-fish-knife complaint and the squared little shoulders. Class will show. *The kid is a prince!*

Our one evening out in Cork was to a local theatre, which featured an Irish show called, "The Flowing Bowl."

There was music and dance and comedy, but the outstanding performance of the evening was the recitation of a poem, "Ode," by Arthur O'Shaughnessy, wherein a poet's spirit is most accurately described.

I thought at the time that two lines in the poem also described the Irish spirit, which, in my opinion, has never been truly understood by much of the world. It's perhaps that many of Erin's sons and daughters have adopted a "life with a light touch" philosophy — bright, successful people who refuse to view life as a Russian play. The casual approach to life is often regarded as frivolous, as though the dreamer, singer, raconteur is "not getting the message." I believe the carefree approach accompanies one who has already taken serious aspects of life seriously and is then free to enjoy the balance of what life dishes up, not growing too Wagnerian in the low periods. The lines I mentioned are highlighted.

46

ERIN

Ode
We are the music makers,
And we are the dreamers of dreams,
Wandering by lone sea breakers,
And sitting by desolate streams;
World losers and world forsakers,
On whom the pale moon gleams,
Yet we are the movers and shakers
Of the world forever, it seems …

… But we, with our dreaming and singing,
Ceaseless and sorrowless we
The glory about us clinging
Of the glorious futures we see,
Our souls with high music ringing
O men! It must ever be
That we dwell in our dreaming and singing,
A little apart from ye.

Outside Killarney we found Burke's Farm in the village of Farranfore, on an inviting hillside setting. Visible from the farm was the Gap of Dunloe, rightfully touted as a "must-see" in Ireland.

Burke's Farm was paradise for Edward. There he found a bosom buddy in the person of Mr. John Burke. They went everywhere together: First to the barn where the cows waited to be milked, then a ride into town where the milk was dropped off at the distributor. In the evening, chores done, the tall, dark, gentle farmer sat for hours at the dining room table playing cards with my lively group.

The gales of laughter were occasionally interrupted by a shout for quiet emanating from Mrs. Burke's bedroom. Quiet prevailed for a good thirty seconds after each plea for silence, but the game went on. I appreciated the masculine attention being lavished on the children who had been fatherless for just a year. Mr. Burke was tall and dark and strong as their father had been prior to his unsuccessful heart surgery. They saw a resemblance and welcomed his love and playfulness. Not many people go out of their way to befriend a child in his or her time of mourning. The few who have done so occupy forever a special place in my grateful heart.

One night, Mr. Burke took the older children into town for a change of pace. He spotted a caravan on the side of the road and immediately spun a wonderful tale about the tinkers who lived in the caravan, having judged his audience accurately.

"You know," he started, "they're not a bad lot, but they're ignored or looked down upon by some. Wouldn't it be lovely if you got outside the caravan and gave 'em a song or two? I'm sure nobody's ever done such a dear thing fer them. You wouldn't be afraid now, would you?"

"Well, what would we sing?" asked Joseph.

"Sure, they'd love anything. It'd be a real treat, you know," Mr. Burke answered, reeling them in. "Would you be knowin' any Christmas carols atall?' That'd be grand. I'm sure no one's ever stopped on the road just to sing carols to tinkers. Good, there's still a light on. Oh no. It's after goin' out. Sing anyway. It'll put 'em to sleep. There you go now. We're right up close to them. Go on now. I'll be waitin' right here. I won't move."

The kids obediently followed the chauffeur's instructions, out of the truck, lined up outside the caravan, they straightened their clothes and agreed on the opening number when Mr. Burke blasted off and left them in the black night to serenade the tinkers. Needless to say, the tinkers were less than entertained, the kids took off along the black road, their hysterics born less of fear than outrageous comedic release.

They found him fifty yards down the road. They burst back into the Burke house that night, uproarious, the architect of the plot the loudest in his appreciation.

The next morning at breakfast, the natives were restless, recalling the events of the previous evening. I understood and listened a while as we continued to eat. When I announced that we'd better finish eating, someone "hadn't heard," so I said again, "All right, that's enough. Mrs. Burke has other things to do. Let's finish, so she can have breakfast chores behind her at least."

One more remark, followed by a snicker or two. I excused myself and crossed the hall to the sitting room where I thumbed through a magazine. Mrs. Burke asked me what I was doing.

"I'm depriving them of my company," I said.

"What do you mean?" she asked.

"Did you hear them acting up awhile ago?" I asked.

"Ahh, it wasn't that bad. They're only kids," she smiled.

"I suggested they eat instead of fool around," I told her.

"Yes, I heard you," she nodded.

"Well, they had to be told again and when that didn't work, I left the table. Apparently they were doing it for my attention. Quiet now, isn't it?" I asked.

"I never thought of doing that," she puzzled. "Where did you learn that?"

"Strictly trial and error," I confided. "Whatever works!"

"More truth than poetry in that!" she said with an appreciative grin. I felt completely at home midst the madness. I can't speak for other nationalities but our Irish-English household, the one in which I was raised, was always filled with fun, either in joke form or some innocent trick planned for an unsuspecting sibling.

For years, the only jokes I was exposed to were Pat and Mike jokes, which poked fun at the Irish. Totally ethnic jokes, innocent and always with a grain of truth. As an adult, I am grateful for that experience. What could be better than learning to laugh at oneself at an early age? I think the world has become a dreary place where each nationality is on guard as it were to be sure no one is saying anything derogatory about the group they call their own. How dull!

I remember a descriptive word applied to anyone who took offense where none had been intended: thin-skinned. It wasn't a flattering adjective. Now the whole world appears to be thin-skinned, everyone poised, waiting for any remark, however innocent, to be interpreted as a slur. Maybe in this new serious world where all are dressed in heavy armor, only a fool would find humor in a Pat and Mike joke such as the following, but the laugh it evoked in my childhood hasn't diminished in my old age.

Many of the Pat and Mike jokes focused on alcohol and its "occasional" misuse. I've never met a Son of Erin who'd deny the possibility, so the simple jokes, which contained a grain of truth, were welcomed with a laugh and another of the same genre the listener just happened to recall. They all started out the same way, "Did ya hear the one about. ..." The Irish are honest enough to acknowledge that the stereotype had strong roots and so what? Good for the Irish! A typical Pat and Mike joke:

Did ya hear the one about old Pat who was drinking heavier than ever? Well, his wife talked to the local priest in desperation and asked for help. She'd done everything in her power to get him to stop, but he wouldn't.

Father McNally listened, nodded, sympathized and finally asked the route Pat took home when the pub finally closed.

"He takes a short cut through the cemetery. I know that for sure, Father," the wife advised him.

"All right, leave it to me then." The priest knew this case demanded extreme action, so he dressed up in a red satin devil's costume, hid in a newly dug grave and waited for Pat to make

50

his nightly appearance. Well, around midnight Pat came strolling along, singing and laughing to himself. As he neared the grave where the priest was hiding, up jumped Father and screamed: "PAT O'MALLEY, I AM THE DEVIL!"

"Shake hands," said Pat. "I'm married to your sister!"

Burke's Farm was familiar although I had never been there before. I often wondered about the strength of the bond between Mr. Burke and our children but I didn't ask. When he played cards with them at night, was he remembering past evenings with his own father? Or did he picture his own children left without his influence for the rest of their lives? He never said, but all through Europe people embraced us and told their stories of having come from large families, or wishing they had many children, or the most popular remark, "You're American and you have nine children? We thought American women had no more than two, except for Ethel Kennedy."

Meanwhile back at the farm, we were convinced that a visit to the Gap of Dunloe should be planned for the next day. When morning showers threatened the trip, Mrs. Burke told us "It's a fine, soft rain" and off we went.

We arrived at the gap, were shown to one of the waiting jaunting cars, which boasted a bench on either side. The driver stood on a sort of step at the rear of the car and I don't remember but I guess the aisle between the benches was for the reins. When we were seated, one group faced the other, except for Mary and Joseph who had decided at the last minute to travel the gap on horseback. I wondered about their choice then and I still wonder about it.

The gap was just that: a sliver of road between two mountains with the threat of a steep drop the only thing keeping you on the path. Off we went, bumping along. At first, my eyes never left Mary and Joe. I gestured and called to them to get way inside, away from the edge.

51

The driver serenaded us with parts of "Johnny's So Long at the Fair." The path fit the car exactly, no margin for error. But error there was. One wheel went a little over the edge. I started moaning. The driver never missed a note until I begged him to "Please stop the damn car. I'll walk! I'll pay you double if you just let us out!"

My pleas fell on deaf ears. "I couldn't do that," he protested. "I'll lose me turn," he said then continued in song, "He promised to buy me a bunch of blue ribbons to tie up my bonnie brown hair."

I still remember the song. I suppose hearing what I figured would be the last song I'd ever hear on earth made an impression. We soon reached Kate Kearney's Cottage where we had scones and tea. At least if the car were to topple on the way back, we'd all die with a good taste in our mouths.

The day of departure from our home at Burke's Farm arrived. Edward begged me to leave him there where he was so content and to pick him up when we had finished touring England and Europe. The answer had to be "No." I think Ed had found such a strong role model with whom he had formed an instant bond that the parting would be wrenching regardless of the time. With luggage secured on the roof rack, we started to say our teary goodbyes. Mr. Burke kissed each of the children as did his wife and we kissed their little ones.

"Goodbye, goodbye. Safe trip. God bless you," filled the air and all but the man of the house watched us leave. He looked at the full van, shook his head, bit his lower lip and burst into tears. He waved weakly, took out his handkerchief and entered the farmhouse.

Too Soon

In early December 1963, the older children had a holiday from school, a Holy day. We had two stops to make after Mass: Joseph's doctor's appointment in Teaneck, New Jersey; and early Christmas shopping at Packard-Bamberger's, an old-fashioned two-story store in Hackensack, a town next to Teaneck. There, an abundance of affordable gifts would fascinate and please each little shopper.

With our eighth baby due in about a month, I had that wonderful prenatal surge of energy. The air was clear and crisp as we started the promising day with no forewarning of storm clouds — atmospheric or emotional. Both varieties would arrive soon enough: one releasing a welcome, gentle snow; the other triggering an unexpected cloudburst within my heart.

At his office, the doctor examined Joseph's back, asked his patient a few questions and decided Joseph's backache was most likely the result of some recent activity in gym class.

"Look at him," the doctor said. "He could be on a poster for the All-American boy. He's in great shape."

"That's good," I said. "I just wanted to be sure."

"Joseph, you can join the other kids in the waiting room," I said. "I'll be there in a few minutes. I want to pay the bill."

As I turned back to the doctor he asked, "Why are you having another child when you know your husband won't see forty-five?"

In shock and dismay, I blurted out, "No one has ever put a time limit on his life. How does anyone know that?"

"I'm telling you he won't live to be forty-five. Why are you having another child?"

"Because I want another child. If I can raise seven I can raise eight."

The doctor shook his head in disbelief.

We left for the store. I quietly wept as I drove and wondered what would possess a doctor to act in such an insensitive way toward a woman nearing her ninth month of pregnancy. Anne spotted the softly falling tears and asked, "Is Joseph sick, Mommy?"

"No, no, Dear. Thank God, Joseph is fine. All-American boy is what the doctor said," I assured her as I dried my tears.

"Why are you crying?" she asked.

"I think I have a little cold," I said. "My eyes and nose are running."

I shifted the subject, "Here we are at the store. Everyone stay near me. There are a lot of cars in the area."

Inside the store and upstairs, all shopped merrily; squeals of delight filled the air. Each one in stage whispers confided which gift was for whom, exuding pride in his or her excellent taste.

"Do you think Mary will like this?" Edward asked.

"Look what I'm getting for Joseph," Anne said.

When I was overcome by the doctor's death sentence, I would hide behind upright display shelves to let the tears have their way, then try as best I could to share in the children's happiness.

I picked up wrapping paper so we could label and wrap the gifts before the temptation to keep the gifts for oneself became too strong.

Back home, one at a time, a child with his or her bag of treasures sat with me at the dining-room table as each gift was held on a lap for wrapping — in case a passerby would dare sneak a peek. Labeling could then be accomplished on the tabletop.

The notion of early shopping, wrapping, labeling and stowing of Christmas gifts was extremely efficient. In general, I am not efficient. I have completed tasks, reached goals, finished what I started, but always in my own time. Often my clock wasn't the one the rest of the world was using. That's fine. No one had to tell me to stop to smell the roses or watch a magnificent sunset. I was doing that sort of thing as the world rushed around me.

This stab at yuletide efficiency backfired, big time. Within a week of our shopping trek and the hiding of gifts, this is how it all played out.

Edward did not like Joseph's attitude toward him, which meant Joseph was unworthy of the model plane Edward had chosen especially for him.

Joseph's gift for Mary, because of a slight on Mary's part — real or imagined — would no longer be hers on Christmas morning.

No sir. That yo-yo would go elsewhere.

Piles of used, wrinkled gift-wrap mounted, along with labels and good cheer.

Note to myself: No more early anything.

After dinner on the evening of our shopping venture, when all were bathed and settled in bed, Bernard and I retreated to the living room, he with his coffee and I with my tea. I sat on the sofa with the newspaper for a prop and a shield when I needed it. Bernard sat in a white leather chair across the room as he announced that there was a good movie on television: "*Father of the Bride.*"

He watched the film and I watched him.

Tonight, at forty, he looked healthy and happy. Could the insensitive doctor's estimate be accurate? I turned the question over and over again in my mind.

As the film progressed, he laughed and asked aloud, "Will I have to go through this five times?"

His rhetorical question found me hiding behind the newspaper and thinking, "No, dear, not even once."

I cried a lot that night while he slept. The next morning he drove me to the hospital. I was in a strong, steady labor, which ended as a false alarm. Three days later on Friday the thirteenth of December, I returned for the real show. Peter arrived a full month early.

President Kennedy's assassination three weeks prior to this had traumatized the nation and each one of us individually. He was so young, so vibrant, and so dear to us that his death had shaken us to our depths. The nation mourned and few spoke of anything else. A nation of people knew what every other person was feeling. There was some comfort in that.

There was no comfort in the dire prediction concerning Bernard's life expectancy. It was a cruel, unnecessary blow, too blunt and too callous to produce anything but anguish. And it was an anguish I bore alone.

Peter had decided to brighten our Christmas season with his early arrival. This beautiful new life lifted my battered spirit from morbid depths to a soaring gratitude. Peter's effervescent personality can still do that.

Perhaps early Christmas shopping, wrapping and such had not gone well but this fabulous early Christmas gift, Peter, was such a blessing that I unilaterally, on that day, initiated the Early Christmas Gift precedent.

It is a policy still in effect 43 years later. Once the gift has been given, the recipient is allowed to use the gift at once — hang the painting, wear the article of clothing, show off the piece of jewelry or cash the check immediately.

Enjoy the gifts you've been given and appreciate them all the more because you have been given that much more time to enjoy them.

I put my spectacular early Christmas gift, Peter, under the tree.

York

I rapped at the door.

No one answered.

I peered through the window.

A boy of fifteen stood in the kitchen, holding a feather in his left hand as he drew his right hand over the feather repeatedly from one end to the other as though attempting to clean it. Strange, I thought. Apparently answering the door was not his job. He stood there, as a woman sporting knee socks, a white lab coat, a topknot and half glasses at the end of her nose opened the door. She was his "Mum."

Yes, there was room for ten to spend a night or two. Immediately following introductions, she informed me that her husband was a drug addict, but it was all right. No need for alarm: He worked at the hospital in order to be near the source of his next fix when needed. "Fix" is most likely my word, but the idea is the same.

She explained socialized medicine over tea. It all sounded so civilized. One has a drug addiction? By all means supply him with drugs whenever the need surfaced thereby eliminating drug pushers and attendant crime. What about helping him kick the habit? Could she live with this situation for the rest of her life? I wondered but didn't delve. We were only guests, after all.

The day we were leaving York was interesting.

"Mum" invited me to have another cup of breakfast tea and a scone before traveling on. There was a method to her madness.

While I sipped, her son appeared in the kitchen. She appraised him as for the first time, starting from the top of his head to his feet and back again. The tasty scone took second place to the scenario that played out before me. It was a vertical viewing of a verbal ping-pong game.

Mum: "A shame you become terribly ill in the car! Isn't it?"

Anthony: "Well, I did, Mum."

Mum: "Don't you still? I imagine that you would."

Anthony: "I don't think so, Mum. I'm a bit older now, you know."

Mum: "Would you like to be going off with them this morning?"

Anthony: "I would, Mum."

Mum: "Well then, put a few things into a bag and off you go!"

Anthony: "Right, Mum."

With the match over and Anthony busy packing a few things, two facts came to mind:

First, I'm still waiting for "Mum" to ask me if I were even remotely interested in one more passenger.

Second, and more puzzling, was the ease with which she relinquished control of and responsibility for her only child to a perfect stranger.

My first thought was that she wasn't free to travel, tied as she was to the B and B. This group of happy "Yanks" presented an opportunity for her son to have some summer fun. That was understandable but I drew the line when she walked us to the VW bus, counted seats and said, "There's room for still another passenger besides Anthony." I don't recall the 1968 equivalent of the current "Later," but I said it and off we went — with Anthony.

For reasons unknown to me, then and now, Anthony brought a tent along with the "few things" Mum had told him to "throw into a bag." Why a tent? Even the tinkers traveled in caravans! Anthony was with us for a few days. He absorbed all the silliness a van full of American kids threw his way. Soon he was indistinguishable from the rest.

Several events occurred in rapid succession. The hotel at which we stayed had a strange method of metering parked cars. A fellow guest had noticed that his auto with French plates was consistently ticketed in the morning but ours with German plates was not. What could I tell him? I was only passing through. What a lousy sport! He told me he had called the police and so we grabbed our belongings and left. On the way out of town, a truck sideswiped our vehicle rather gently. I didn't pursue it. The police already had our license number.

Suddenly, things were less than serene. Anthony realized we were traveling at a good clip to anywhere far away from there and asked about a possible destination, how far it would be from home and so on. Who knew? He knew his way home at this point so we dropped him at an entrance to the underground, quickly, complete with tent. Unceremonious, but efficient.

I recall sending comics to their address for his father, at his "Mum's" request, and I believe Anthony dropped us a note. At least he didn't hold a grudge!

Nottingham

Thoughts of Robin Hood filled our minds as we approached a lovely bed and breakfast. The proprietors were as elegant as the appointments. We'd never have known how gracious and interesting this couple was were it not for a need that surfaced after most of the children were already asleep.

Anne needed something to take the edge off cramps. We quietly went downstairs and sort of whispered our plight to the lady of the house. She asked if the children were asleep and when I told her that they were, she said there was no reason to whisper. She was right. I thought perhaps a warm drink of some kind would do the trick. Her husband brought out a bottle of brandy, which not only took away Anne's pain but did the same for the adults as well. It was one of those wonderful, unplanned moments whose warmth will never fade.

It could have been as simple as handing us two pills, a glass of water and a cheery "good night." For that, we would have considered ourselves fortunate. But a first refusal of a "wee drop" on my part led to, "well maybe just a drop." Straight liquor didn't appeal to me, but after all, these gracious, caring people offered a special treat, not merely a sedative. How could I refuse? One taste led to another, as did the stories we exchanged.

Their spellbinding war stories, about experiences we in the States had been spared, were easily told now more than twenty years after the events, with life back on an even keel. Of course there were tears, but they were greatly outnumbered by shared laughter and sips of brandy. I don't recall how long we lingered, but morning came sooner than expected, not with a rude awakening, but with a warm remembrance of newly forged bonds, intimate though temporary.

The breakfast table was set with fine china, crystal and silver. The entire short stay spoke the words "cherished guest" to each of us.

When we left and all had piled into the bus one more time, our genial host appeared in the driveway and stopped us shortly before a narrow lane at the exit. "Woman driver" was the first thought that entered my mind. I was certain he felt compelled to guide me through the narrow exit. That would have been all right with me: Femininity and driving confidence would never be threatened by a caring gesture.

I was surprised when he motioned for us to stop.

I rolled down the window to say another goodbye. He took my hand and said, "It's been a pleasure to meet you, my dear. In the future when I'm down about something, I'll simply think about you and all my troubles will disappear."

My ego screamed, "Wow!" But my mouth most likely said something simple like, "Oh, how sweet. Thank you."

Olivier had nothing on him. This fellow could deliver a line!

* * *

Mary and Edward had created an odd little dance that ended with a light touching of right eyelash to right eyelash. A woman observed their most unusual choreography and asked, "Are they disturbed?"

"Extremely," I answered.

Nodding toward the rest of the group, she asked, "Are they all disturbed?"

"To one degree or another," I said.

"Are they related?"

"By marriage."

"What role do you play with the group?"

"I'm taking them for a ride through parts of Europe," I said.

"Alone? Are you doing this alone?"

"Yes, I'm the chauffeur, counselor and guardian."

"I hope someone is paying you well for doing this."

"Oh, I'm not getting paid."

"What? That is a disgrace. Why isn't someone paying you for such exhausting work?"

"Think about it. What should anyone be paid to do this job?"

"That's right. You're right. How could anyone ever pay you enough?"

"No one could. No, this is a labor of love."

"Well, God bless you," she said

"Don't you mean, 'God help me?'"

"Well that, too."

The sweet benediction from a total stranger had bolstered me. When the woman left the scene to rush home and share with her family the story of the strange encounter, I gathered the dancers and their cohorts into the bus. Once all were inside and seated, I shared with the American ambassadors the great impression they were making.

Reactions varied.

"Mommy, how could you say we're disturbed?" Liz asked.

"The word disturbed never came out of my mouth."

"As our mother you should have corrected her," Edward said.

"Look who's talking? You inspired her questions with your strange little dance. Anyway, she didn't know I was your mother."

"You lied to her?" Chris asked.

"Not really. She asked what role I played with the group. Role means part. I am playing a lot of parts: chauffeur, counselor and guardian."

"And mother," Mary added. "Why didn't you tell her you're our mother?"

"She didn't have all day. I think she had to catch a bus. Who's hungry?"

R and R

"I have something to tell you. Sit down," Bernard said as I walked into the house carrying Peter. We'd been to the pediatrician's for Peter's last diphtheria shot.

"That sounds ominous," I answered.

"First, how's the baby?" he asked.

"Wonderful! Couldn't be better. He had his last shot for a while. Didn't even cry."

"That's my boy," he beamed. "Here, let me take the baby, sit down."

I really don't like surprises; usually one person's idea of a great surprise falls flat when presented, ruining a sweet gesture for all involved.

"Okay, I'm sitting, so ... ," I started.

"We're going on a Caribbean cruise," he blurted out.

"Who is?" I asked.

"You and I, from April fourth through the fifteenth: it's all arranged. We'll have the tickets in a few days," he said as he waited for my reaction. "Well, say something."

"Wow, I can't believe this," I said. "A cruise. I haven't got a thing to wear."

"I *knew* you'd say that. So, go clothes shopping tomorrow," he chirped.

The whole idea was out of character for him. It was a loving thought, no doubt, but the truth was my emotions were *very* mixed. Weighing heavily on my mind and heart was the question of time: would his condition deteriorate rapidly or could there be years ahead? Whatever my deep feelings dictated, I could not pop this magical balloon he had extended.

"Where did this come from?" I asked him, still shocked.

"I've been thinking about it for a while but I thought it would be best to wait until the baby was four months old or close to it," he answered. "I remember how you enjoyed the cruise to Bermuda with your friends when we were dating."

"There's nothing like a cruise. It's a lovely surprise. Thank you," I said. "Now give me all the details. What's the name of the ship? From which pier do we sail? I thought we were buying a new station wagon. Is this instead of that?"

"No, I called Joe to order the car." He asked, "You wanted white exterior and red interior, right?"

"How are we going to swing all this?" I wanted to know.

"Let me take care of that," he suggested. "We have a lot of other plans to make during the next couple of weeks."

"All right, it's all yours," I said, still thunderstruck. "I'm still amazed at all of this."

"Peter is asleep. I'll put him in his crib," I offered. "Look at him. Isn't he magnificent? You know he's the best baby we've ever had."

"Therese, you say that about each baby," he laughed. "Think you're a *little* partial?"

"Maybe just a little," I said.

As I put him in his crib, I wondered how I could be away from him for eleven days. A cruise taken in my early twenties with friends was a laugh-a-minute experience, in carefree, oblivious youth. This was another story. He had made reservations after much thought for reasons that were apparent, rest and a change of scene for both of us and perhaps for deeper unspoken needs. How could I refuse?

We sailed on April fourth from our appointed New York City pier: relatives with our children in tow waved us off, but Anne, our oldest at twelve, cried inconsolably as she waved. I felt like joining my dear little friend on the dock. I really didn't want to be anywhere but home.

The first two nights I retired at a normal time, however my escort said I was missing the best part of the cruise: While I slept most passengers danced then enjoyed a midnight buffet. Two good nights of sleep were sufficient. We danced every night after that, danced, ate, had a drink or two and I wondered why I had worried about this fellow, king of the wicked rumba.

One morning we sat poolside on deck, swam for an hour then took a short cut through the bar to our stateroom. Bernard sat at the bar, patted the bar stool next to him as an invitation. We sipped strawberry daiquiris and giggled when the bartender answered our question about the time — it was ten thirty *in the morning*. Bernard was more relaxed and completely different than I had *ever* seen him. It was as though we had just met.

Soon after departing New York, passengers mingled, most trying to find others matching their social status or maybe a step higher. Since he intended to be alone with me, he got the whole thing straightened out pronto.

An attorney and his wife introduced themselves. Of course the first question was directed to Bernard, "And what do *you* do?"

With a straight face he responded, "I'm a bookie."

A nervous cough and grin was followed by, "Do you have children?"

"Yes, we have eight children," the rumba king answered.

"How long have you been married?" asked the gentleman whose profession is interrogation.

"Oh, we're *not* married," he said. "In fact, the reason for this cruise is to decide whether we're truly compatible."

Case closed. For the remainder of the cruise we were alone together just as he had planned.

I had grown up in a large family, relating to many personalities at the same time was natural for me. He grew up with one sibling, a dear brother whom he had lost during World War II. He preferred one-to-one, quiet, serious relationships. I relished a healthy mix of people hopefully with a fine storyteller or two thrown in to enrich that mix.

A simple choice made in Howard Johnson's soda fountain one summer afternoon played a spotlight on our distinctly different personalities. Immediately he decided upon a vanilla ice cream soda with vanilla ice cream while I was paralyzed with possibilities — *twenty-eight* flavors from which to choose. Wonderful! Black raspberry, butter pecan, chocolate-marshmallow I read with delight, asking him as I read, "Did you see all these flavors?"

"Uh huh," he answered, "quite a selection."

"So, how come you're ordering a plain vanilla soda with vanilla ice cream when there are so many more interesting choices?" I wanted to know.

Quietly he answered, "I know what I like."

On the cruise I had bits of conversations with a few interesting people whose company I could have enjoyed, so many "interesting flavors" of personalities all with their own stories. But "plain vanilla" wasn't having any of that.

One character in particular, an Art Carney clone, introduced himself and his wife the first day out. He wondered what we intended to buy on the islands. His wife mentioned a shop on St. Thomas that carried a vast array of cuckoo clocks. They glanced at each other and then burst into laughter, which rendered them helpless.

R AND R

Bernard looked at me and shrugged as a way of asking what could be this funny about cuckoo clocks. I was willing to wait for the story.

She explained that a cuckoo clock had been her heart's desire on an earlier cruise.

"So did you find one you liked?" I asked.

"We found a beauty, just the right size, complete with little flowers, mushrooms and tiny animals at the base. It was a perfect … ," she reminisced.

"Do you still have it?" I asked.

"Well, sort of," she grinned.

"Is it still working?" I needed to know.

"It was well made in Germany," she explained.

"She made a big mistake when she hung it in our bedroom," Art complained. I'd had a disagreement with a guy at work one day. He ended up calling me a cuckoo. That night I was still a little upset, tossing and turning. When midnight rolled around that damn bird taunted me with his first three chirps. I wasn't gonna take nine more squawks, so I threw a shoe at it."

"Makes sense to me," Bernard agreed.

"I still have it, well most of it, in a box in a closet," she said. "I never did find the little deer and one mushroom."

The following morning I stopped to see the ship's medic; I felt a little seasick. He asked me to describe my symptoms. I used my only frame of reference, similar to morning sickness, I told him. He smiled and nodded approval.

I ran into the woman who had shared the cuckoo clock story; her eyes were swollen, she hadn't slept all night. She had left her husband with a group of partiers around midnight, with a casual, "See you later."

"I've been up all night praying for him," she said. "He must have fallen overboard. What else could it be? He's never done anything like this before. I can't believe it."

"Have you seen any of the people he was with last night?" I asked.

"That's the first thing I did this morning," she sobbed. "The magician who put on the show last night told me he left my husband about three a.m. as they both headed to their staterooms on different decks. I know he's gone. He's crazy especially when he drinks, but he always comes home."

"Perhaps. ..." I started, when who should sheepishly approach but Art in the flesh, his only drowning having come from a bottle.

"Hi-ya, hon, I'm sorry," he started. "Jeez, I tried to find our room but I think I was on the wrong deck. I don't know how I ended up in a different room; I heard people talkin' in the hallway then I see a boat go past the porthole, I didn't know if it was 'abandon ship' or what the hell it was. I jump out of bed, go runnin' up on deck in my bare feet and underwear."

I excused myself, having no desire to be called as an eyewitness to whatever action was about to ensue.

Lunch for me was saltines and tea; I was certain that by dinner the queasiness would subside.

On the island of St. Kitts we took a box lunch and headed for the nearest park, a short walk. We sat on the grass and were about to eat when a native woman appeared. She didn't speak but held out her apron as she pointed to our plentiful food. Bernard looked at me and suggested we give her four pieces of fruit included with our lunch.

"Sure, honey, that's a good idea," I said as I handed her my contribution with a smile.

There were still no words coming from her, only another gesture toward what was left of lunch, two huge sandwiches, salads and lemonades. One glance from Bernard and a nod from me left us lunchless. That was fine. Her last gesture was the most amusing; she pointed at the boxes — her apron was full.

"That was sweet of you to give her our lunches," I said.

"It was nothing. Did you see how her eyes lit up at the sight of all that food?"

"I wonder if she was mute," I said. "Of course one look at the empathy in *your* eyes spoke volumes, language would have been superfluous."

He wondered aloud what happened to the excess food on the ship, hoping the answer would be that it was shared with hungry islanders. As we got up to walk around the park he laughed as he speculated about the destination of our lunches, maybe the quiet one had re-packed them for sale. Who cared? In either case she would have profited from his generous gesture.

Shortly after boarding the ship, we passed our "man overboard" acquaintance, who spoke briefly about his escapade from the previous night.

"That guy was a magician all right," he said. "He made my fifth of scotch disappear in half an hour!"

As we approached the University of Puerto Rico, a laden mango tree greeted us. Mango is my favorite fruit. I picked one and relished every juicy morsel as I concluded Eve was a pushover in the Garden of Eden. She fell for an apple. Every woman has her price: I know I'd have been a paragon of virtue beneath the apple tree; the mango, however, would have been a different story.

As we traveled and shopped the islands, souvenirs for the kids were paramount, except for one afternoon on St. Thomas, when Prince Charming ushered me into a jewelry store. He thought he'd like to buy me an emerald. A mango fresh from the tree and now an emerald? I protested for a few minutes, but when he said it was something he really wanted to do, much like the mango episode,

71

how could I resist? We looked at many beautiful stones, but just as "plain vanilla" knew what he liked, so did I. Although there is no comparison in value, I chose a forest green oval tourmaline with two diamonds set in eighteen carat gold. I dubbed it "My spoiled rotten ring!" The cruise that I had questioned in my heart when the subject first came up was a fabulous idea: Eleven days completely removed from all responsibility, with no time to ponder the inevitable, was superb therapy.

The night of the fourteenth, our last night at sea, foghorns blasted madly. It was eerie and frightening. While we danced the music had drowned out the sinister warning. When we returned to our stateroom I said to Bernard, "Someone has locked the porthole cover in place. I don't like this."

"It's nothing," he assured me. "Just a precaution they take when it's foggy."

"I'm going to find someone to ask about this," I said. "What if we don't get home tomorrow?"

"I had the same thought!" he grinned impishly as he danced me round the room, "What if we *don't* get home tomorrow?"

The foghorn had ended my reverie with the thought of eight *orphans* at home while he had remained in the fun-and-games mindset.

I slipped out to the stairway where I met a crewmember most likely assigned there to assuage normal apprehensions.

"The foghorns, covered portholes: are we in danger tonight?" I asked, hoping he spoke English better than most of the crew.

"If portholes covered on *Andrea Doria*, lives would have been saved," the *Angel of Death* proclaimed.

"Foghorns are … are archaic. They're, ah, old," I stuttered. "Isn't there something like radar for a time like this?"

"Yes, we have but," he said.

"But what?" I demanded.

R and R

"The captain no sure how to use. No sure," he answered.

"Great … the captain no sure," I mused on the short walk back to our cabin. "Well maybe the captain no sure but *I'm* sure we're all going to drown!"

"Honey, you're never going to believe this!" I said as I entered. But Honey was already fast asleep. I looked at him and thought of the statement, "A coward dies a thousand deaths; a brave man dies but once." No contest here: he's sleeping peacefully and I'm working on my second thousandth death. What a match!

I hung up my dress, put on a nightgown while contemplating the details of the last few hours left to us on this earth. It's April, therefore the water temperature will be low. Would fog make it warmer? No, just impossible to see. Okay. If there is no lifeboat available for a while, I think I could float and swim. I've always been a pretty strong swimmer. Oh, but what's the difference if the water's too cold?

While I pictured flotsam and jetsam in the ice water that will kill me, I recalled the first slightly off-color joke I had ever heard since my setting was the same. (The joke is better spoken rather than read, since a high, affected voice is essential to the best delivery, but I'll share it, nevertheless.)

A wealthy woman had bought a parrot from sailors on an island. Sailing home, the ship hit something and sank. Mrs. Smythe found herself bopping around in the sea, wondering what had happened to her expensive purchase. After a while she spotted him floating on a piece of driftwood.

"Polly, oh Polly," she called, "I'm over here."

"Hi, Mrs. Smythe," answered the bird. "How's your ass?"

Embarrassed Mrs. Smythe replied, "SHUT UP!"

Polly said, "So's mine! Must be the salt water!"

The healing gift of laughter had plucked me from death in the briny deep. I snuggled next to the *voice of reason* whose protective arm was always there.

All that strong swimming in frigid waters had tired me. As I was about to doze off, two exciting facts entered my mind: the foghorns had stopped and in a matter of hours I would see my babies again.

I reached up and scratched the rumba king's head. I was rewarded with a smile in his sleep. I looked from his peaceful face to the spectacular ring, knowing it would always serve as a reminder of sun-filled days and music-filled nights: The honeymoon we had postponed for fifteen years. The ring, however, paled in comparison to John, our last baby, who had kept his presence a secret for a few weeks and was a quiet, welcome stowaway on our cruise.

Who needs jewelry when she can have a real live gem? Not me!

Neither of us could explain a phenomenon that occurred when John began to speak; he called himself "Captain John!"

John's always had a way with words!

Stratford Upon Avon

Home of Shakespeare, what a thrill! A treasured find at Hathaway's cottage, the complete works of the bard on parchment-like paper for somewhere around a pound. It was one of the few items not stolen from the van when we left it in Barcelona to be shipped to the States.

An all-time high for me was attending a performance of "King Lear," last row in the theatre, with acoustics so good not a syllable was lost. Doubly enjoyable since we had recently dissected Lear in class.

While Anne and I waited in line for tickets, we had an interesting conversation with a man directly in front of us, a solicitor no less. He was a local who never missed a performance and was most generous in sharing with us his vast knowledge of Shakespeare, presenting theory as theory and fact as fact. Would one expect less from a gentleman whose profession is law? He was very dear.

He assured us that he would wait to be sure we had secured seats. If we hadn't been successful he wanted us to use his tickets. Sounds a lot like someone you'd meet on Broadway!

The bed and breakfast at which we stayed in Stratford was like a little theatre. The man who owned the business had been married once before. The unfortunate ex-wife was now in a psychiatric facility, although he gave it a less gentle name. The second wife, who was in residence, he had wed because she was a really good worker. Who said romance is dead in England?

The "good worker" sort of spooked around the house, just appearing out of nowhere. Her body was present, but her mind had long-since checked out. She loved the young children and spent lots of time with them, sitting on the floor, playing with their Matchbox cars, laughing and chatting merrily. The minute I appeared on the scene, she'd jump up and run from the room as though she were frightened of me. That would have been only fair since she scared the hell out of me more than once.

The landlord had asked me at breakfast if I'd mind switching one of our rooms. He explained that two of his regular guests had requested the boys' room — their favorite for some reason. I pictured a sedate British couple full of reminiscing in their favorite room. No problem, I assured the landlord, who offered to move the boys' belongings later that morning. I simply had to remember the number of the boys' room had changed from 5 to 7. What I hadn't remembered was to advise Joseph and Edward of the switch. Time enough for that.

Edward, at eleven years old, came back to the house after an afternoon watching model boats on the Avon. He also came back before I could tell him of the room switch.

He ran up the stairs and swung open the bedroom door, expecting to see familiar faces. Instead he encountered two men and a woman, au naturel, enjoying a pillow fight. Just as he noticed an empty champagne bottle, one of the pillows broke open spilling feathers everywhere, blocking the occupants from view. Edward, however, was still very visible to at least one of the men who, still in his natural state, decided to chase him part way down the hall.

Luckily both "shows" — "Lear" and the one Ed had seen — let out at about the same time. I met Edward at the end of the street. We walked "home" together as he breathlessly told me of the strange encounter. Entering, my eyes did a wide sweep for errant feathers. No feathers in sight.

Just then, however, the proprietor floated down the staircase holding the hand of a woman he introduced as his girlfriend, who also claimed this as her residence. *Ménage à trois* all over the place!

I had the distinct feeling the proprietor received special rates at the psychiatric facility: An ex-wife was already institutionalized, her successor (the "hard worker") was well on her way if behavior is the sole predictor of such things.

Dinner conversation was spirited that evening, all interspersed with the following: Avon, floating feathers, marathon runners in loincloths of terry and the genius of Shakespeare.

Those were the voiced thoughts. When my mind wandered back to our present lodging arrangement, I kept my thoughts strictly to myself and took great solace in the simplicity of widowhood. Among other things, it was wonderful to realize that, as a widow, I could never be replaced. Did that qualify me as irreplaceable? Of course it did. Technically, at least.

"Irreplaceable." Ah, that word has a lovely ring.

Time for dessert already? Of course. Order anything you want! When a woman is certain that she's irreplaceable, the sky's the limit!

John

"I have a doctor's appointment in Teaneck this morning; I hope it's the *last* one," I mumbled.

"You must be tired of waiting for this baby." Bernard then asked, "What, is it close to three weeks overdue?"

"Today it's nineteen days past my due date," I said. I answered trying hard not to complain to him who had everything to complain about but never *did*. "I am a little tired but not bad. I just don't know why. I feel out of sorts."

"What time is your appointment?" he asked.

"Ten thirty," I sighed. "By the time I shower and dress it'll be time to leave."

"Take a long shower and try to relax," he soothed. "No need to rush."

"I'll try. I'm sorry I'm just a little anxious," I apologized.

"That's all right. The sitter will be here at nine thirty. I'm glad we don't have to take the kids with us today."

"They're no trouble, but today. ..." I trailed off as I went downstairs.

The phone rang. I called back to Bernard to pick it up since I refused to answer one more call that started with, "Are you still home?"

The sitter had instructions and assured us that she had no demands on her time for the rest of the day so we didn't have to rush. Good news.

The thirty-minute drive was quiet except for the last ten minutes.

"Today is January thirteenth," I broke the silence.

"The thirteenth, right," he agreed. "Pete was born on Friday, December thirteenth," he recalled.

"He broke that silly superstition of bad luck connected with Friday the thirteenth," I mused. "He's such a blessing. That was thirteen months ago today come to think of it. Wouldn't it be funny if this baby arrives today, two thirteenths thirteen months apart."

"If it's a boy, I'd like to name him John Peter after my grandfather," he said. "Do you like that name? He was a seafaring Norwegian. In those days wives traveled aboard ship with their husbands."

"John Peter," I tried it out for sound. "That's a good strong name. Is there some connection between this child having accompanied us on the cruise and naming him for a sea-going relative?" I laughed.

"I hadn't thought of that," he said.

"Wonderful thing, the subconscious mind," I observed as we pulled up to the office door.

"What if the stow-away is a girl?" I wanted to know as Bernard opened my door and helped me out of the car.

"We have time to think about that," he finished.

"Go right in, dear. Dr. Fox is on today," the receptionist said.

A handsome Irishman greeted me with a hand up on the table, the same doctor who had told me at our first meeting that I was knocking myself out having babies in rapid succession. He questioned the wisdom of it all. I shared with him that we wanted a large family: It was all right, no cause for alarm.

"You've been in labor for hours," the good doctor told me. "Go across the street to the hospital. Dr. Higdon is on duty today."

JOHN

"I can't believe this. I haven't had even a hint of labor pains. This is incredible." My mood changed from glum to festive.

I had heard Dr. Fox's family was growing at a rapid pace, much as mine. I couldn't resist. As I stood to leave I asked, "So how many children do you have now?"

The number he gave was six or seven I believe.

"So what happened to that fellow who told me I was a youngster knocking myself out having many children like so many steps and stairs?" I demanded to know.

Typically Irish, he didn't miss a beat. As he approached the door, leaving the room, he said, "Well, you get older. …" turned with a wicked wink and added, "and wiser!"

At the hospital, dressed in a hospital gown, I was welcomed by Dr. Higdon. He always said goodbye after a birth with, "Come back in a year or send a friend!"

I reminded him of his parting words. He smiled and called me his "little perennial." He had the perennial part right, but little I wasn't.

John's birthday was unusual from the start. Whoever heard of labor without pains? No complaints from me on that score. Labor without pain? I was giddy at the thought.

Settled into bed in a labor room, I had another gigantic surprise: Bernard sauntered into the room with Dr. Higdon. Thinking back to eight other dramas similar to this, I believe I told Bernard he wasn't supposed to be there. I had always referred to labor and delivery rooms as "no man's land." This was the drill at Holy Name Hospital during the fifties and sixties: Husband bid a fond farewell to his wife outside the doors of the labor room. She entered the inner sanctum, labored, delivered and husband was told the vital statistics, i.e., boy/girl, weight, baby's and wife's condition, then in due time he was invited to visit wife who was now resting in an ordinary hospital room.

Bernard in the labor room? What would Sister Canice, supervisor of maternity, have to say about that? Where was she by the way? This ever-present figure was nowhere to be found. Her absence made me a little nervous. She ran a tight ship. I dreaded the thought of her coming in and ordering Bernard out. This was no time for a scene. Dr. Higdon said he would be showing Bernard around labor and delivery, advised me to relax, everything was fine.

So I relaxed in an incredulous state, aware of my surroundings, and why I was there, yet I expected at any moment to awake from this experience and be told I had merely dreamed of labor minus pain with my husband present in the delivery of our last baby.

Dr. Higdon smiled at the two of us, quietly chatting, and announced that he was going home for lunch, but would be back shortly. He waited long enough to share a little story with Bernard. First he looked at me, laughed and said, "You know, Bern, she was a real witch this time. Last week in an office visit, she looked at me very seriously and demanded to know, 'What's happening with my baby?' I excused myself, went to the files and returned with several records of women who were also quite late. I called out their names and due dates to ease her mind that she was not alone in this wait. You know what she said? More serious than before she told me she didn't care what was happening to anyone else, only what was happening to *her* baby. Imagine that? I was just trying to be kind and sympathetic."

All three of us laughed at the truth revealed, and then the good doctor left for lunch.

Bernard read a newspaper. I closed my eyes and wondered.

Dr. Higdon returned, checked the progress of my labor, and said it was time for the delivery room. I could not understand any part of this procedure. Not a twinge, not a moment of discomfort and now this child's birth was minutes away. Beyond a gift, it was a total blessing. The good Lord has His own way of doing things. If Bernard was to witness one birth, in his weakened condition, he would have felt helpless in the company of a wife suffering those pangs, so He blessed all three of us with quiet and peace and a painless childbirth.

I was given a shot just prior to sliding onto a gurney for the trip across the hall to the delivery room. What a shot that was. I have no memory of the twenty-foot ride. I do recall the doctor saying, "Okay, sweetie, slide over onto the table."

I answered agreeably and returned to my knocked-out state.

"C'mon, Therese, slide your hips onto the table," the doctor coaxed.

"Okay," still cooperative, I answered as I opted for la-la land once again.

"*Therese!*" Dr. Higdon ordered. "Get over on the table. If you can't do it, I can move you, but if I do, I won't have strength left to deliver your little baby."

I moved.

Eventually I opened my eyes and saw no one in the delivery room. No baby crying his first cry, no doctor, no nurse. This never happened before. Strange, very strange.

I took a deep breath and looked up at the lights over the table — they had been turned off.

I looked down. Someone was holding my right hand. I looked to the right at someone in green scrubs, seated on a stool next to the delivery table.

"You look just like my husband," I said.

"You look just like my wife," Bernard answered. "You should see the baby, he's a handsome little guy."

"Really?" I asked. "So John is here. Today is the feast of the Baptism of Jesus and John baptized Jesus. No wonder he kept us waiting — he chose today as his birthday. Now I understand."

A short while after I was settled, a woman whom I had met when we first arrived, came to my room. She told me she had delivered a son also, there was a problem with the baby's blood, but she wasn't upset because the problem was being addressed immediately. Then we discussed the special day on which our sons had been born. She said she had looked through the delivery room door while I was giving birth. At first I thought it was a strange thing to do, only because I wouldn't have done it.

"The reason I'm here," she said, "is to tell you I watched your husband during and after the delivery. He had an expression on his face that is indescribable."

"I know that look," I said. "It says, 'I love you, thank you, I am so relieved that you are all right.' I've seen it after each child was born, no other time."

"Well, I had to tell you because I've never seen that look before. I have three children and I can tell you my husband's face never glowed like that. It was special."

Proud but somewhat embarrassed by her statement, I offered, "I'm sure your husband admires and appreciates you and tells you so. With men of few words, one must be adept at reading expressions."

We wished each other well.

A few days later, we took John home to Swan Street, where in the company of our eight other blessings, we celebrated life and love every day.

London

Like all good tourists, we had to watch the changing of the guards at Buckingham Palace.

When we had finished watching and discussing tradition, the younger kids wanted to run through Saint James Park. Why not? It was a beautiful day and a good run through the park could take the curse off sitting and standing in the bus for hours at a time. If they had been at home, they'd have been running and swimming all summer, seldom in the car for more than a few minutes at a time.

"Run, tumble, have fun! Don't cross any streets and don't pick the flowers!" I called after them. I wasn't far behind but I lost sight of them momentarily when we exited the park. A brick sidewalk ran in front of a series of brick homes, which were, I assume, occupied by worthy retirees of the Queen's service.

I had told them not to cross streets and not to pick the flowers, but what I hadn't cautioned against was in full swing as I turned a corner.

Thérèse had decided to challenge one poor guard's routine march back and forth before a particular residence. She first stood toe to toe with the impeccably turned-out soldier, tall black bearskin hat and all, even in July, wordlessly daring him to move.

Undaunted, he took a sharp step to his right, she to her left; nothing had changed. Now he stepped to his left, she to her right. He said, "Excuse me, love." Taken aback, she cleared out of his way.

She marched at his side and mimicked his drill to perfection. I turned the corner at the fourth pass and found a disciplined military man, strongly resembling the snappy guards we had watched minutes before at Buckingham Palace. The only difference was the tears running down his cheeks and the scarlet tinge to his face as he earnestly tried to stop laughing.

"Thérèse, what are you doing?" I asked.

"Marching with my friend!" she replied without missing a step. At the corner, in perfect sync, they turned, the guard and his buddy from the States.

Movie camera in hand, I called, "Make this your last time, honey. The other kids are already on their way to the bus." She left with me reluctantly, marching as she smiled back at her new friend. Winks were exchanged and off we went.

Back in the bus, Thérèse voiced her frustration at being cooped up by shouting her three favorite words out the window as we drove.

Parents often boast about their offspring. In this instance I'd love to boast about the words she chose to scream. "Gee, golly, wow" would have been bragging material, at least acceptable material. She had chosen instead, "shit, bastard, hell." She knew they were bad and she used them to full effect when she was angry: "Shit! Bastard! Hell!" I couldn't help but wonder how her friend in the bearskin hat would have liked that!

Nobody could pin such behavior on ugly Americans: There was a huge D for Deutschland plastered on the rear of the bus. Wherever we went in Europe, when the air turned blue with swearing, the best one could assume was that there was a German child in the Volkswagen bus swearing out the window in English. It worked for me! This left our roles as ambassadors intact.

The host at a bed and breakfast had assured us that we'd find London "smashing." We did indeed. Mary was smashing Ed; Ed was smashing Joe. The high spirits necessitated three crossings of the London Bridge before my charges took notice. On the third go 'round, I shouted above the babble: *"Everybody look, damn it! This is the London Bridge and I'm not going over it again!"* The passengers became so many tin soldiers, upright in their seats and silent, until Chris observed, "Nowhere near as good as the George Washington Bridge!"

So American and so right!

Dean's List

"Thank God everything's quiet and it's only nine o'clock," I said. "I have a philosophy paper to write. Would it bother you if I sit here at the desk to study and type?" I asked Bernard, who was resting nearby on our bed. "I could go up to the dining room, spread books out on the table if I'd be disturbing you here."

"No, that's all right," he said. "Stay where you are. I'm pretty tired so I think I'll be asleep soon.

He asked, "Do you think you'll make the dean's list this semester?"

"I don't know. I hope so. We'll see. Do you want anything before I sit down?"

"No thanks," he said. "I'm fine. Just tired. Don't worry about me. Just get to whatever you have to do."

"Okay, Soren Kierkegaard, Danish and 'leap of faith' are all I know about this one. Let's see, I have plenty of resource material. That's good. I'll read, take notes for tonight and hope I have time tomorrow morning to make sense of the whole thing before I type the paper. Here we go!" I said aloud to myself in the form of a little pep talk with some loose planning thrown in.

"Therese," Bernard started, "I feel really cold. Before you start studying, could you get me a sweater?"

"Sure, honey. How about this maroon one with the zipper? When you warm up, it'll be easy to slip it off while you're lying down. I'll rub your back a little before you put the sweater on, no extra charge!"

"Oh, that's much better. Thanks," he said. "Now you'd better get back to the books."

"Right. Philosophy is something I'd like to delve into someday when I have unlimited time. At the moment, most of it eludes me since my time to *ponder* is spent on mundane thoughts like laundry, food preparation, chauffeuring, homework, settling arguments."

"And taking care of me," Bernard added.

"That's my pleasure!" I reassured him. "Okay, back to the great Dane."

"Therese, my feet are freezing. Could you get me some warm socks, baby?"

"Sure. How about the long, gray ones? They're the warmest. Too bad we didn't keep the argyle socks I knitted for you when we were first married. Remember them?" I asked, knowing what his response would be.

"Well *one* of them would have warmed me up to my knee. The other maybe to my ankle," he recalled.

"So they didn't match! Big deal! They were a labor of love, all those bobbins to watch and stitches to count. It wasn't easy!"

He shook his head while I rubbed his feet and pulled on the *matching* long gray socks.

"There, that should do the trick," I assured him as I returned to the desk.

"All right, philosopher and theologian," I read.

"Therese, I'm sorry to bother you, but I'm still cold," he said.

"That's all right, sweetheart. Maybe you need warming from the inside. How about a large mug of hot chocolate?" I suggested.

"Maybe that would work," he said.

"I'll go up to the kitchen now. Want marshmallows in it?"

"It doesn't matter. Just make it fast," he pleaded.

Out of our bedroom, into the hall, up several stairs and through the dining room I had less than charitable thoughts.

"Dean's list?" I scoffed. "Only if she has two lists; and my name will appear on the less favorable one, the one that doesn't start with D!"

As I watched the milk heat, I mixed cocoa and sugar in the bottom of the mug. Slowly I added milk to make a paste before adding the balance of the milk to the mix, tossed in marshmallows to cover the surface, dropped the pot into the sink to soak, flipped off the kitchen light and started my return trip to Bernard and Soren in that order.

"Here we go, dear! Just what the doctor ordered," I chirped as I entered the bedroom.

He was fast asleep.

I tucked the down comforter around his still body. "Sweet dreams," I murmured.

That night I made an interesting discovery: Philosophy is more easily swallowed with large gulps of hot chocolate, marshmallows optional.

Paris

The lights of the city gently twinkled a welcome from a short distance.

"Hurry, call Anne and tell her that Paris lies straight ahead. She won't want to miss this. Ah, how exciting, Paris!" commented the driver.

"She won't wake up, Mom," Edward said.

"Well, then shake her, damn it! This is Paris!" Every light in the city is ablaze. Do you think they're expecting us?" I asked with an air of adolescent self-worth.

"Maybe the man in the last store alerted them, Mom, after you acted so funny," Liz suggested.

"What was so funny? The language barrier prevented me from a simple purchase, underpants for the girls. I resorted to body language."

"Yes, but. ..." Liz started.

"I simply pretended to have a pair of panties in my hand, made the motions of putting in one foot at a time and then to be sure he understood I went on to pretend I was pulling them up. What else could I have done? Really?" I pleaded.

"Well then, how come he brought out a girdle from under the counter?" Liz wondered.

"Well, they both go on the same way. I finally pointed to all five girls and he brought out five small girdles and gave me the strangest look," I continued.

"That look wasn't as strange as the one he gave you when you pointed to the window. He really looked upset, kept shaking his head and saying 'No,' sorta through his nose," she added. "Anyway, why were you pointing to the window?"

"Because I finally spotted a sample of just what I wanted in the window," I answered.

Thérèse, always most perceptive, cracked the case wide open with her usual brevity. "It wasn't strange at all," she explained. "The salesman thought you wanted to try on underwear in his window. I think we got out of there just in time. He kept looking at the phone. I think he was gonna call the police. Anyway, before we left home, didn't you say you wanted to buy yourself a dress in Paris?"

"It was a thought," I said.

"Then why didn't you do that instead of trying to buy us underwear and almost getting arrested? I don't understand you at all," the seven-year-old added comfortingly.

"Well that's all behind us now," I sighed.

Chuckles from the back-seat crew indicated they had found great amusement in the use of the word "behind" when the discussion had so recently centered on underwear. Thank Heaven for the little touch, of getting fun from nothing much.

Anne of the sleepy eyes had now joined the living and focused on the lights below. If her heart shouted, "Ooh la la," her face kept it a secret. She stared ahead silently, the calm that I have since learned to cherish. It's always so brief.

Joseph, nearly fourteen, announced authoritatively that since Anne had done such a fine job of running to strange doors in search of bed-and-breakfast accommodations, he would do the same in France.

"Oh great!' Anne responded. "How much French do you know?"

"You know that I don't know any! But you could teach me a few phrases I'd need. Like, how do you ask if they have room for ten people?" Joseph queried, his Leo leadership quality asserting itself.

"Oh, that's neat. You're just going to run into each house or hotel and ask those few little words? Go ahead. Lots of luck!" she replied. No French lessons today!

"Now, Joseph," I started. "Don't you think it would make sense for Anne to continue what she has been doing so well, especially here in France?"

"There's no reason why she has to be in charge all through Europe," he answered.

"Well it's not really being in charge. It's more like being responsible for one aspect of the trip. Think of it that way. You and Edward have been doing a great job with luggage. I appreciate that," I explained.

"But I could do even more than that to help," he offered.

"Great! So what else would you like to do?" I asked, innocently enough.

"I'll arrange for hotel rooms," he answered.

None are so deaf as those who will not listen.

The luster of Paris faded in a flash. It started to rain. Members of the bed-and-breakfast brigade, heads held high, stared out opposite windows. What a scene! Exasperated, I pulled over to the curb on the Boulevard St. Germain and as neatly as I had maneuvered the bus I set myself in stage posture, shoulders back, head tilted upward, I started to share my less-than-tender thoughts with the passengers.

"Well, isn't this grand?" delivered with a dramatic sweep of the right arm for emphasis. "Here we are in ... ,"

Just then, a disheveled woman approached the bus and upstaged me in the gesture department. I joined my former audience in open-mouthed astonishment. She stood at a relaxed sort of attention and saluted. The dramatic pitch, which I had begun with such determination, was now scrapped. As the stage posture melted into a sliding slouch behind the wheel, my dramatic speech gave way to a "Now hear this" approach.

"Listen to me! I'm not fooling. This is very serious. Look straight ahead. Pretend she's not there. Don't laugh!"

"Mommy, who's that funny lady? Hi, funny lady," greeted friend John, laughing from his three-year-old belly.

"John, look straight ahead. Don't laugh at the poor lady. She looks very sad. You don't want to hurt her feelings, do you?" I asked.

"No, Mommy. Maybe she would cwy. Oh look! Hewe she comes to the window. Ha, look at her funny shoes! She's a clown, Mommy!" he announced gleefully.

"She sure looks like a clown," Mary encouraged, as Pagliacci's long-lost French cousin crisply saluted. She missed the mark. Her thumb landed on her nose. Perhaps it wasn't a salute after all!

Mary joined in John's laughter.

"Mary, please," I begged. "Oh God, I wish I were home!" I moaned.

"I'm not really laughing at *her*. I'm laughing at *John* laughing at her," explained Mary.

"Go ahead, Mary, go right on laughing. If she decides to throw a rock through the window, she's on your side!" I said.

For a while, all was quiet. Enter Anne, our friendly interpreter, whose high school French reassured me considerably. Our curbside friend was saluting and blessing us profusely while the other side of her mouth cursed de Gaulle and blamed him for her sorry state. She cursed Charles as she gestured toward her feet, which sported one shoe and one sneaker. He was also to blame for her bloodshot eyes. Her shoulders lifted as her lower lip protruded, Chevalier style. I expected a song. Now that I knew she had blessed us, I relaxed. As she discussed the bloodshot eyes, which Charles had caused, she held each eye wide open between a thumb and index finger as she bent closer to the window of the bus. Her approach caused most of the passengers to lean toward the street side. The only two holdouts? Mary and John.

John beamed through the window, thanking her with his eyes for delighting him and the single smile she managed was exclusively for John, her biggest fan. Mary's mood had turned to pensive as she surveyed the reddened eyes.

"Are her eyes bloodshot from crying, Mom?" she asked.

"Most likely," I answered.

96

"Uh oh, can you get 'em from drinking? She's drinking something out of a paper bag. How can a paper bag hold liquid?" Mary wondered aloud.

"It can't. Inside the bag is a bottle no doubt," I said.

"How do you know? Did you ever drink that way?" she asked.

"No, but George Washington told me that he did!" I laughed.

"Mommy, did you *really* play with George Washington when you were a little girl?" asked Thérèse.

"Every day after school!" I answered.

"I'll bet that Gall she's talking about is her husband," Mary announced. "And last night they were drinking and this morning their shoes and sneakers got all mixed up and they each ended up with one shoe and one sneaker."

"Mary, the Gall she's talking about is Charles de Gaulle, president of France. I'm sure he enjoyed wine with dinner last night, but wherever he is at this moment, I'm sure his eyes are clear and his shoes match," I suggested.

A friendly gendarme led the woman away but she delayed her departure long enough to deliver one weak salute to the bus in general and a sweet "au revoir" directed at John with a smile and a tear. John responded in kind, a smile, a wave and a happy "Oh wah, funny lady!"

The cold war in the second seat had defrosted to the point of Anne volunteering to hop into a cab, explain our lodging needs to the cabbie and arrive at an appropriate hotel. We'd follow close behind. Simple enough. Agreed! Very often the interpreter comes up with very clever ideas. The cabbie knows Paris; he'll find us the best. ... Where'd he go? What a crazy idea, letting Anne hop into a cab in a foreign country with someone I've never seen.

"There they are, Mom. Go as fast as you can. At least we'll get the license number in case we lose them for good!" consoled Joe.

"Everyone hold on. This can't be any worse than driving in Manhattan," I hoped.

"Speaking of New York," moaned Edward, "I wish I were back there, playing baseball in Palisades. Besides, Billy's mother was taking him to a big amusement park and she said I could go with them."

"She's a good mother," Joe chimed in. "Every year she takes the kids there. They go on every ride. This year we could have gone with them."

"Yeah, could have, 'cept for this dumb trip to Europe," Ed agreed.

"Chins up fellas. You've been to amusement parks many times. Our trip to Europe is more than half over and someday you'll re-member it fondly and maybe return when you're older," I coaxed as I sped after the cab in which my first-born rattled through the streets of Paris with a total stranger.

"Not me! Never!" Ed assured me.

"Me neither! From now on, for the rest of my life, I'm gonna swim and play baseball all summer like *normal* people do," Joe declared.

Meanwhile we passed all the "must-see" attractions Paris has to offer … twice. Mario Andretti's French counterpart pulled to a stop in front of the hotel he recommended. As Anne paid him and offered lavish thanks, Mary observed that the ride had been fun, but it had ended directly across the boulevard from our starting point. Score one for the French cabbie!

The street was quieter now and on that quiet note we entered the Studia Hotel on the Boulevard St. Germain, settled into four rooms and soon the children were bathed and happily asleep.

I opened the French doors, stood out on the balcony and said to all of Paris, "Here we are, you lucky people!" I breathed deeply, backed into the room, shut the doors, hopped into bed, and smiled in the darkness as I thought about tomorrow.

"London is a man's town
There's power in the air,
Paris is a woman's town
With flowers in her hair."

Early the next morning, after placing a few sprigs of Lily of the Valley in the girls' hair, I realized the truth of those lines. Paris *felt* gentle, even in the volatile summer of '68. It appeared that all couples held hands, young and old alike. Romance was alive and well and living in Paris. Or was I more acutely aware of couples in the newness of widowhood? *Mais non!* Paris and romance are one.

"But when it comes to living, There's no place like home" ends the poem. True as that may be, Paris wasn't a bad second and I wasn't ready for the end of the poem just yet.

Our days were filled with the usual tourist pursuits, special only to us. The illuminated bus tour of Paris proved enjoyable for all ages.

"April in Paris, chestnuts in blossom,

Holiday tables under the trees," I sang, savoring the reality of Paris.

"Isn't this July?" Chris asked Mary, who sat admiring her hair-do in the mirror.

"Yeah, it's July. Why?" Mary answered.

"Then how come Mommy's singing about April in Paris?" Chris whispered.

"You know Mommy. Time isn't important to her. Maybe she planned on being here in April and by the time she arranged the whole thing it was July," Mary suggested.

"Or maybe there's no song about Paris in July," Chris kindly suggested.

"There's nothing to do here. At least if we were home we could play baseball," Ed complained.

"I know how rough it is for my two older men. The babes are napping, the girls are gabbing and if you had a good mother, she'd have taken you to an amusement park," I sympathized.

"It isn't that you're not a good mother," Joe said, "but I told you I didn't want to come to Europe. The only reason you forced Ed and me to come on the trip was 'cause if we stayed home and the plane crashed and you died, we'd be orphans. Isn't that right?"

"Right!" I snapped.

"Hey, I didn't know we had a choice!" Ed reacted. "I'd rather be an orphan!"

Time for some serious righteous indignation! With shoulders squared, left hand on hip, I turned swiftly and started, "Well, isn't this lovely? I've heard nothing but complaints from you two since we left home. Will you ever forgive me for dragging you through Europe and away from a dusty baseball diamond? Believe me, my pitiful, persecuted little men. ..."

I addressed them and, gleaning fire for the delivery of the punch line from their contrite expressions, I attempted a magnificent sweep of my right arm to punctuate the point when shouts from the street below sent my less-than-rapt audience running to the windows.

The French scene-stealer had returned to interrupt my best dramatic attempts. Right then and there I retired that sweeping gesture. It served no purpose but to beckon Madame Salute. By the time I got to the window she was again being led away.

"Why don't we buy her some shoes?" Thérèse asked.

"Forget that. She'd probably leave them at Charlie's house again," Mary quipped.

In Paris for three short days and already she's calling the president by his nickname. This group doesn't mess around.

"Well what can we do?" asked Ed, now the spokesman for the forlorn Little Leaguers.

"Here, take this money and map. Use your imaginations. The Metro entrance is on the corner. Bye-bye," I said. They took the challenge and left. I gave them fifteen minutes, tops.

Anne returned that afternoon from a three-day bus tour of chateau country and delivered many interesting tidbits as only a breathless sixteen-year-old can. First, the director of the tour had announced the itinerary and, predicting cool evenings, requested a donation of a sweater for an American girl who had boarded the bus naked. Actually, Anne wasn't naked at all, but she hadn't packed warm enough clothes and the tour director was trying to help in his own French way. The French have a word for sweater-less, but he chose another word — the word for naked.

No one offered a sweater, but she had provided the fellow passengers with a good laugh to start the tour.

When the tour ended, in an effort to quickly return to our hotel, she tossed her bag into a waiting car, jumped in the back and gave directions to the man behind the wheel. The driver regarded her in his rearview mirror long enough to tell her that he was not a cabbie and this was not a cab: The taxi stand was across the street, he was simply waiting for his wife to come out of a shop.

"Hi sweetheart," I called to John as he awoke from his nap. "Did you have a happy dream?"

"I dweamed of funny lady. I like her. She's my fwiend," he announced as he rubbed his eyes and nestled his curly head on my chest, the same routine his eight siblings had followed, held close and rocked gently into the real world again.

"Why do you let him speak like that? You're a teacher now. You should correct him. When he goes to school. ..." Ed instructed me, as he walked into the room from his afternoon on the town, map in hand.

"Tell me, Ed, anyone ever laugh at the way you speak?" I asked.

"No. Why should they? I don't talk like that," he answered.

A glance, which traveled from me to Anne to Joe to Mary was the cue for us to squeal "Cwazy Cwissie," followed by a burst of laughter. They had read my glance to perfection and recalled Ed's response at three years old to being told to climb up on the bench in the kitchen.

"Not sitting next to Cwazy Cwissie!" was his response.

I had no need to correct every little imperfection on the spot. I assured Ed that by the time John was ready for school, we would have heard the last of "wabbits" and "wocks" and the like. For now, let me revel in the joy of John, my last baby.

Such dear little speech errors are short-lived as are precious baby days. Thank God for the good sense to enjoy every aspect of my childbearing years. Pregnancies. Births. Two a.m. feedings. The works. They were not so many inconveniences to be endured, but one more call to joy after joy. The miracle of a new life who, contrary to women's lib jargon, is not part of a woman's body but a tenant of nine months who needs a warm, protective shelter until he can make it on his own: precious transients, defenseless and dependent for their survival on the size of the landlady's heart.

Liz asked Ed to show her on the map where he and Joe had traveled to that afternoon. He declined. "Why don't you show your sister where you've been, Ed? Maybe you two covered more territory than we have so far. So, where'd you go?" I asked.

"Well, it wasn't too far from here, down that way and over a couple of blocks," he said rather sheepishly as he pointed.

"You've been gone all afternoon and you only traveled a couple of blocks?" I asked.

"That's all we had to travel, we went to a movie," Joe explained.

Anne, jealously guarding her claims to this foreign language, asked, "How could you understand a film in French?"

"It was in English, the one where the Three Stooges … ," Joe laughed.

"Three Stooges?" I asked in disbelief. "You could have seen them at home, couldn't you?"

"Yeah, but we're *here*," Joe declared. Couldn't argue with that.

I explained the plan I had for a smooth departure from Paris the following morning.

"That's funny," said Liz. "I never heard you say you had a plan before."

"That's right. I usually have a very general plan, loose in structure in case something unplanned happens. I don't like disappointment, so I don't get too specific. But this time, I think a tighter plan could work," I said cheerily.

"So, what's the plan?" Liz asked.

"Here's what we'll do. First of all, we won't have breakfast together," I started.

"That's what we *won't* do," Mary jumped in.

"All right, first the boys will go down to breakfast. When they come upstairs, the girls will go to the dining room. When they've finished, I'll have breakfast alone," I said.

"Alone?" they sang. "Without us, Mom? What'd we do?"

How could I explain that I needed this time alone for the uninterrupted pleasure of a fresh croissant and the joy of being served cafe au lait from two pitchers? There was something therapeutic about it. A touch of pampering I felt in need of at that moment.

"That's a good idea," Chris said. "And we'll watch Peter and John."

"Great," I agreed.

103

"I'll show them the key chains I've been collecting and read them Jeremy Fisher and maybe Jemima Puddle-Duck," Mary volunteered.

"Thanks. I shouldn't be more than a half-hour, quick breakfast, I'll pay the bill and be back upstairs before you know it," I assured them.

Our last day in Paris meant one more dash to the Louvre and an evening meal at an outdoor cafe. We lingered over the meal and strolled back to the hotel, chatting happily. The mood was light. As the troops lined up for the elevator, I chided the lazybones for not walking to the third floor. Besides the elevator took only four passengers at a time.

"Wait if you want to," I said. "But I bet by the time you get to the third floor, I'll be resting on my bed." Casually I approached the staircase and, while they watched, I slowly started the climb. Once out of their sight, of course, I ran, counting the floors as I dashed. At the top of the stairs I caught my breath, saw no sign of the "lift" kids and, swinging the slightly ajar door open, I leapt onto the nearest bed.

In mid-air, I saw two Asian people in my room, she brushing her hair and he writing a letter. What nerve! In my room! As I got to my feet, I noticed that the furniture was different. This *wasn't* my room. More startling than my mistake was the calmness of the couple: He offered a Mona Lisa smile and she also smiled as she turned from the full-length mirror. In their position, I'd have screamed and thrown something.

Dilemma. How does a confused English-speaking American woman apologize to an Asian couple in Paris? No problem. I hunched up my shoulders, extended both arms, palms up, smiled, backed out of the room while I said, "Wrongie roomie!!!" I bowed out of the room and, in the hall, knocked over a scrub bucket left by the maid who was preparing the adjoining room for new arrivals.

Exhausted I arrived at my room to shouts of, "We won! We won! We beat you to the room!" The lift kids cheered for themselves.

"Please stop," I begged.

"What's wrong, Mom?" they asked.

"You wouldn't believe it," I said. I told them — and they believed it.

That night, in anticipation of visiting a new country, the girls laughed louder and talked longer than usual after lights out.

"*Mon Dieu!*" he started out and that sounded harmless enough. The complaint emanated from the room between my room and the girls' room. I couldn't hear them clearly, so I depended on his reaction for the degree of their boisterousness. I assigned a score of two out of ten to a simple "*Mon Dieu.*" A screamed "*impossible*" rated a five. When he started to cry and throw things, I ran down the hall and stood in the doorway of the girls' room.

What ailed that man? Angelic was the first word that came to mind as I gazed at several button-smile expressions. Just in case they could hear in their "sleep," I whispered, "Good night, my darlings. I'm going to sleep now. Should there be any further disturbance coming from this room, I shall remove handcuffs from the man next door, loosen his straightjacket and. ..."

"Mommy!" Mary shouted.

"Any questions?" I asked.

"No. We'll go right to sleep. I promise," Mary answered.

As I passed the door of my secret weapon, I heard, "*enfants terrible!*" uttered slightly above conversational tone. Sounded like a *four* to me!

The morning of our departure found the penitents eager to follow our plan to the letter. First the boys ate and returned to their room with nothing more than, "Good morning, Mom." Apparently, the girls had given them the scoop on the previous night's antics and now I viewed guilt by association. Their quiet was abnormal but acceptable. The girls returned.

"Hi, Mom. Joe and Ed said they'd watch Peter and John while you have breakfast. We'll check all the closets and drawers to be sure we haven't left anything," offered Chris. Self-inflicted guilt was everywhere that morning. Delicious!

I entered the dining room alone and was greeted warmly by the Spanish waitress. In her limited English, she told me that the children were very well-behaved. I thanked her and drew my chair closer to the table. I gazed at the boulevard and pondered this planning-ahead idea. It appeared to have merit. The serenity, which had been mine for the first twenty-six years of my life had returned. The thought was as delightful as the brief respite I savored along with the cafe au lait.

Emphasis on brief.

As the waitress poured from both small pitchers at once, I reveled in the glories of motherhood, travel and freedom. I attributed this euphoria to the fact that I had taken a minute to plan our orderly departure a mere twelve hours in advance. Mental note: Try this at home. Plan ahead!

Lights suddenly flashed behind the front desk, a horrible gong sounded, interrupting the thought, which could have changed my life forever. Or, was I saved by the bell from leading a life devoid of spontaneity? The waitress dropped the rest of my breakfast and dashed in the direction of the elevator, shouting, "*Bambino*, patron, lift, *por Dios*."

Since I was the only guest with a *bambino*, I followed close behind. There was John, smiling a "Hi Mommy," while his head was wedged between two balusters.

"John, take your head out of there. Where are your brothers? Your sisters? Why are you here alone?" I asked.

106

The Spanish waitress was crying and holding her ears, the Asian couple smiled, and our French friend from the adjoining room was the patron whom John had stuck between floors by pushing all the buttons at once. I had to revise the scale of madness! One to ten was inadequate. He was emitting at least a fifty and, from the waitress's hysterics, a benediction it wasn't! Add to this interesting group John's mother who would at that moment have sold him to the highest bidder. But who'd want a child with a neck as long as John's was sure to be once he was free?

Many people offered help but I feared letting any of the volunteers get their hands that close to his neck. Inspired by the curses shouted from the lift, I freed John and together we hurried upstairs, away from the scene of the crime. The screams met us at each successive floor and I thought even *curses* sound better in French. Beautiful language!

Chris reported that all closets and drawers had been checked. Mary offered that she sympathized with the chambermaid and had helped her strip all beds. Liz and Thérèse played with the dolls they'd been collecting and the New York Yankees arrived to tell me that John was missing.

"He was here a minute ago," Joe said, "playing on the floor with his Matchbox cars. Oh, there he is. Have a nice breakfast, Mom?" he asked in relief.

"Yeah, *peachy*," I answered.

I quickly checked the rooms and marched the troops downstairs. At the front desk all was quiet, lights had stopped flashing, the gong had ceased, and in this silence the manager stamped the bill "paid," bowed and smiled — just as he had when I flew into his room in error. Was the bow a sign of respect or was he stooping to be sure I held John's hand? Maybe he imitated my exit bow from his room? I'll never know.

He carried John to the bus, seated him and returned for Peter. This time out his wife and the maid followed. They insisted upon loading the luggage onto the bus, then stayed on the sidewalk until we were out of sight. All three waved handkerchiefs furiously. The Frenchman from the lift wasn't there, but three out of four wasn't bad.

"Wasn't that kind of them to help us with our luggage?" Liz asked.

"Yes," agreed Thérèse, "and the man was kind to carry Peter and John to the bus."

Chris wondered about their having stayed outside the hotel until we were out of sight.

"Mommy, was that because they *really* enjoyed having us there?" she asked.

"Why, of course," I lied. "They *loved* us in Paris."

Maurice

"You're up bright and early on a Saturday morning," Bernard noticed.

"And wide awake! Maybe it's going to snow! Now if I start washing windows you can be sure there'll be a change in the weather," I laughed.

"You fall asleep faster than anyone. I've heard of someone falling asleep in the middle of a sentence, you fall asleep between good and night."

"Clear conscience," I assured him.

"We should get the freezer back today, probably this afternoon. It's taken long enough. It was supposed to be back last week. I can't believe they've been waiting a week for a part."

"It's been all right, with the extra freezer in the garage," I said.

"If you don't mind the gaping space under the refrigerator. It's ugly," he said as he passed.

"It's temporary. Let's have a fire," I suggested, changing the subject.

"A fire?"

"Why not?"

"It's 6 a.m. What's with you?"

"It's different, a change of pace. I'll get some kindling and a few logs from the garage. Want to roll some newspapers? They're on the hearth."

He walked into the living room shaking his head, most likely wishing I'd slept late. Who needed an intrusion on his early morning solitude?

"Br-r-r, it's pretty nippy in the garage," I said.

"Seventy two in here. Sure you want a fire?"

"I'm sure," I said, as I put the logs on the hearth and the kindling into the fireplace. "Fires are magical. Wait till you see the reactions from the kids. They'll love it!"

"Especially the oldest one."

"Anne?"

"No. You!"

I smiled in agreement as I watched the fire start.

"Now, isn't this cozy and wonderful?" I asked.

"You'll never be older than eighteen, Therese."

"Is that bad?"

He smiled as he shook his head one more time.

110

"Remember the day we decided on the fireplace? We were in a store on Route 17, looking at used brick for the exterior of the house."

"You thought new brick looked cold and institutional," he remembered.

"Well, it does. It's all right on banks, libraries and schools, but it's not homey."

"While I looked at bricks you looked around at fireplace possibilities," he recalled.

"I think we'd considered a brick fireplace but I turned a corner and fell in love. I'd never seen one like that before. I asked the salesman all about it then couldn't wait for you to check it out. At the time, I didn't think we'd own such a work of art. I only wanted to show it to you."

"Royal Tennessee marble, random widths, seventy dollars a ton. I remember it well. I thought it was a good price. There was no doubt in my mind this was the *only* one for you," he said. "It was doable. Mr. McKenna was sure that he and his sons could construct it for us. The part you never saw was how it looked just dumped in the dirt. They had to cut each piece according to a plan. Fifteen feet wide, wall-to-wall, ceiling to floor, marble. What a job."

"The McKennas were artists. They sent the hearthstones to Massachusetts to be polished. You chose great craftsmen to build our house, sweetheart. The brickwork and plastering is superb. Not a crack anywhere."

"You sound like a construction company commercial."

"And for you, my love. Thank you for such a beautiful home."

"First the fire and now this. What's going on?" he asked.

"I don't know. Save this memory for the next morning I arrive in the kitchen, one eye open, making barely audible sounds."

"I think I'll make hot cereal for the kids," he said. "By the way, honey, guess what they complained about recently?"

"Give me a hint," I asked.

"They said my hot cereal wasn't like Mommy's 'cause it didn't have any lumps in it."

"I have brainwashed them to believe hot cereal's more nutritious with lumps. You didn't *change* that notion did you?"

"Never," he said, putting my mind at ease.

Squeaks and squeals and breakfast by the fire was the order of business that morning.

References to *camping out, pioneering, olden times out West* all surfaced as the natives enjoyed lump-free Wheatena. Had the scene played out at the kitchen table, we'd all have missed a great start to Saturday. To show their appreciation, the kids put on a little show for us, using the raised hearth as a stage.

"Hello, hello, hello. We hope you'll like our show!" each show always began.

"There's a truck coming up the driveway, Bernard," I observed. "It's probably the man with the freezer. He's alone. How will he manage by himself?"

"I'll take care of it," he assured. "Keep the kids out of the way while he brings it in."

"Everyone stay in the living room while the man brings in the freezer," I called.

"Bonjour, Madame," our visitor greeted me.

"Bonjour, monsieur," I answered, bringing a smile from him and a questioning glance from the master of the estate. There will be a discussion about *this* later for sure, I thought.

"You look like Maurice Chevalier," I said.

He took a funny little bow. Maurice and he had been friends in their youth, or so he said.

Bernard who had supervised the installation of the freezer stood with a check in his hand. This is how *he* saw things: There was a job to do; the job was done; a check was given to the service man who immediately vacated the premises.

Frequently life was not that cut and dried. This was one of those days.

Maurice's buddy admired the house and the children as he sauntered into the living room. He ooh la la'd at the fireplace complete with embers, then stepped up on the stage so recently vacated. He sang several ditties all in French while he danced a few steps. He welcomed applause from the children and me. I did not welcome the pained expression on Bernard's face. There would be an inquisition when the show was over.

Inside, I roared with laughter at Bernard's reaction to this eruption of entertainment. I knew the form the questioning would take. I also knew I had to keep a straight face while I offered an explanation he would *never* buy.

Maurice of the protruding lower lip left with children as his escorts, waves of appreciation accompanied him down the driveway.

"Therese," Bernard started, "come here a minute, please. I have something to ask you."

"Uh-oh," I thought. "Don't laugh. Get the smile off your face. Okay, a deep breath. Here we go."

In the living room, I joined him on the sofa.

"So, what's the question?"

"Would you mind telling me what happens to people when they come into *this* house?"

"What do you mean?" I asked.

"You know what I mean. The guy who just left. All he had to do was bring in the freezer and put it in place. But, nothing's ever that simple in this house, is it?"

113

"You mean his little act?"

"Yes, that's exactly what I mean. Why did that happen?"

"He liked the children. Maybe he doesn't have any. I don't know. I didn't ask him to perform. It just happened."

"Why'd you tell him he looked like Chevalier?"

"Because he did."

"I'm sure he knows that. He's probably heard it a thousand times. You didn't have to tell him. You didn't have to say *anything* to him."

"Hey, I'm a Mommy not a mummy! I thought it was fun."

"Anne, did you understand anything our little friend sang?" I asked as she passed through the dining room.

"I didn't understand all of it but in one song he said, "For a quarter I'll show you my backside, for a dollar I'll show you the rest," she translated.

"Pretty cheeky!" I said, pun intended. "Lucky it was in French."

One more shake of his head as he left the living room, and the warmth of the morning faded into our memories.

"I'm going to rest awhile," he said. "Maybe we'll go for a drive when I get up."

"Okay, dear. Sleep well."

"Poor Daddy," Anne said, and then we both burst out laughing.

"Tank heaven for littoo gails," I aped while I danced around the kitchen.

"Yeah," Anne said. "Why didn't he sing that?"

"That could have been his encore. Maybe next time."

"Next time Daddy will pick the freezer up at the shop rather than having it delivered," Anne suggested. "Did you see how he looked while that man sang and danced? He didn't like it at all."

"I thought it was a pleasant little interlude."

"You and Daddy are not at all alike," Anne observed.

"In many ways we're not. You're right. He's serious. I'm light-hearted. I like spontaneity, he likes things that are planned."

"So, why did you marry each other when you are so different?"

"Opposites attract. Being in love with someone doesn't mean you must be the same as that person in every way. That would be boring. We have our own distinct personalities, our own likes and dislikes."

"Are all married people that way, so different from each other?"

"I don't know about all people, but I've observed it in many couples. It's not bad; that is just the way it is. In fact, when I meet God, that's the second question I'll ask him."

"What question?"

"Lord, why did you make men and women so different from each other that mutual understanding is nearly impossible?"

"What's the first question?"

"Why mosquitoes?"

Nuremberg

Strange feelings and quiet thoughts accompanied our departure from Amsterdam. The Frank House wherein a family had hidden, sacrificed, suffered, hoped and had finally been betrayed, was still very much with us as we drove. I assumed my deep soul-searching was connected with having lived through that period in history.

The children asked many unanswerable questions: the existence of evil in the world, man's inhumanity to man, and opportunity for flight prior to occupation were a few of the topics covered. Discussion was lengthy; answers were few.

Strange to leave the temporary hiding place of a family in Amsterdam and enter the nation whose maniacal dictator had made hiding a necessary way of life for many. Transformed from a free, human life to a nocturnal animal's existence was a terrible fate, yet the strong will to survive evoked deep gratitude for the opportunity to do just that.

As we neared the German border, I was filled with unease. I believed it was a carryover from my teen years spent during WWII, years filled with large doses of daily propaganda and statistics of war dead and wounded, presented as so many numbers when reality told an entirely different story.

"Killed in action," "missing in action," "wounded in action" screamed headlines after a major engagement with the enemy, military jargon, which translated into telegrams of dread delivered to individual homes across America, changing families forever. Such telegrams were impersonal as they delivered the most personal of messages, which began with those damnable words: "We regret to inform you. ..."

A mother read, wept as her mangled heart attempted to put the fact into human terms. The son she bore and cherished and delighted in, the child she taught to be strong and loving and kind, the son whose greatest joy was to make her laugh and make her proud has left her life as he lost his life in some remote area of the South Pacific or in a place whose name may be familiar in what was dubbed the European Theatre of Operations.

What's the difference where? The question in my young mind was always *why*? Useless, senseless war, a game wherein all countries involved sacrifice their finest potential, their precious children. Among those lost forever in that war were my beloved brother, Francis X. Powers, and my would-have-been-but-never-was brother-in-law, Edward I. Kramer, Bernard's brother.

Twenty-three years after the end of WWII, driving toward Germany, my thoughts erased the years but not the sentiments on the futility of war.

Anne, who at sixteen had put herself in the place of the other Anne, interrupted my unhappy reverie. She was nauseous, she said. She had been deeply touched when she read Anne Frank, *The Diary of a Young Girl*, but was overwhelmed by the experience of occupying the same space in which the heroine had hidden.

"How could the German people have been so cruel?" Chris wanted to know.

"Well it wasn't *all* German people. It was the Nazis following Hitler's orders who did those things," I tried to explain.

"Why didn't the Nazis tell Hitler they wouldn't do such mean things?" Liz asked.

"It's not anything I can possibly answer," I confessed. "I wish I could. Experts in human behavior, that is — why people act in certain ways — can't explain such evil. I certainly can't."

"Did all of the Nazis think Hitler was right? Is that why they obeyed him?" Ed asked.

"No, not all," I explained. "There were some brilliant German generals who knew Hitler was out of his mind. They planted a bomb near him at a meeting hoping to end his life."

"Is that how he died?" Mary asked.

"No. Sorry to say the plan failed. He lived to continue the evil he had begun. He committed suicide in a bunker when Germany had been defeated," I added, hoping to end the discussion.

"What's a bunker? Is it a place with bunk beds?" Thérèse now joined the discussion.

"No, Thérèse," I said. "It's an underground building where Hitler was hiding with his girlfriend, Eva Braun. He married her just before they both committed suicide. They made sure they wouldn't be taken alive."

"So, Hitler wasn't brave, was he?" Ed observed.

"No, not at all," I said. "A bully isn't brave, whether he's a dictator of a country or a nasty kid down the block. When the tables are turned and someone's about to pay him back for what he's done, he runs or hides."

"Or kills himself in the bunkhouse!" Thérèse added.

"Not the bunkhouse," started Ed.

"Close enough!" I ended the topic.

At the German border, an unsmiling guard asked if I spoke German. I answered in the one German word I knew. He scrutinized our papers, stated that ours was a nine-passenger vehicle and there were ten of us. The ball was in my court.

I smiled and said, "I could leave one of the children if you'd like."

He smiled, raised his hand and loudly answered, "Nein! Nein!" then waved us on.

"Or 'Eight! Eight!' if you keep one of us here!" Joe stage-whispered.

"Was he a Nazi?" Liz asked. "And why did you say he could keep one of us?"

"No, he wasn't a Nazi," I reassured her. "The end of the war ended the Nazis. He apparently takes his job very seriously. I joked about leaving one of you because I wanted to see him smile."

Suddenly Peter shouted, "Sprachen zie Deutsche?" a perfect imitation of our friend, the border guard. Because we were totally amazed at the perfect rendition by four-year-old Peter, the bus was once again filled with laughter. Such positive reinforcement was not wasted. His question was repeated many times throughout the rest of our time in Germany, always getting a laugh.

We stopped at Nuremberg. I explained that the trials of the Nazi war criminals had been held here. Again we discussed the fact that the average citizen of any country is not the one making decisions concerning war and for the most part, whether at home or abroad, people are good.

We stopped at a bed and breakfast and were shown lovely rooms. The last room, where Joe and Ed would stay, was at the rear of the house and down one level. There were bars on the windows, which I thought strange.

One of our little pep talks about being good ambassadors was apparently *overdue*. The owner delivered a little talk concerning the lack of manners on the part of tourists as she glanced from child to child. Of course, American children were mentioned in a less-than-favorable light. I listened politely for a while, but found it difficult not to respond when she repeated the fact that American children lacked good manners.

Confrontation is disagreeable to me, but she was attacking two of my favorite groups, Americans and children, in one fell swoop. I maintained steady eye contact with her. I wanted to say, "Listen, lady ..."

Instead I assured her that not *all* American children are ill-raised. She smiled at the reassurance, and at that *very* moment, Edward ran the length of the twenty-foot room and landed on the top bunk ... shoes and all. Despite this, she rented us the rooms.

"You're right, Mommy. Most people are good. She could have said, 'See what I mean about American kids?' but she didn't," Chris said.

"Edward, come here please. I think you've forgotten something," I started.

"I'm sorry, Mom. I have the top bunk at home and I wanted to be sure I had the top bunk here," he said.

"Ed, with your shoes on? You wouldn't do that at home. Why here?" I asked.

"Well, you and the lady were talking so long about whether American kids have manners, I just got tired of waiting. It was a nice, long run and I was sure I could make it to the top bunk in one jump. Besides, aren't there any athletic ambassadors?" he wondered.

"Grant me patience," I prayed as we walked to the front door where the owner invited us in to sign the guest book. She wished us a pleasant stay.

As was the case in each place we stopped, the hostess asked about the absence of a husband and father. I explained briefly. She shared some of her background over hot chocolate and cookies. Her story was *far* more fascinating than mine.

A relative in her distant past had been the mistress of Lord Nelson. In exchange for her "devotion," he had bequeathed her the use of a castle somewhere in England, which gift would include all of her heirs and descendants down through the ages. This had to have been the inspiration for *Let's Make A Deal!*

Everywhere we traveled in England, there was a column with a statue or bust of Nelson atop. Had she been responsible for the number of such? When you think about the deal she got, it was the least the frau could have done.

The last day we were in Nuremberg, we bought two beautiful clocks at a factory store recommended by our hostess. We had dinner prior to returning to our rooms for the night. Our new friend was disappointed; she had prepared dinner for us. Such a sweet gesture.

The clocks are now Ed's, both of them. It wasn't a generous gift from a loving mother, but a constant reminder of the "bunk bed/shoe incident."

Ah, guilt! The gift that keeps on giving.

Shopping

In the several years prior to his death, Bernard was extremely weak at times.

I don't know why weakness came and went. I would have assumed, knowing little about medical conditions, if the heart is malfunctioning he should have been weak every day.

Some days he ascended five stairs normally, bad days the same stairs took at least five minutes to climb. The best I could do was to take it as it came and pretend not to notice him as he stopped on each step. That's what he preferred. That's what I did.

Some days he felt well enough to volunteer to pick up groceries. He knew he didn't have to, but doing so when possible improved his view of himself. These shopping expeditions were a source of pride for him in another way. He made a list, stuck with it and was home in whatever time limit he had allowed that activity, usually less than an hour. He was a good shopper. Actually he was good at everything he did, efficient and precise, a perfectionist.

What a laughable coupling of people! His shopping list was in his hand, mine was in my head. Occasionally, when I *had* taken the time to make out a list, I'd leave it on the kitchen counter. At least writing the list had refreshed my memory as to necessary purchases. I didn't want to burst his bubble concerning my casual shopping habits but I did have a plan, however loose. First I shopped for meat. Then I created menus as I strolled the aisles. As I strolled, I thought of each Kramer's food preferences and tried to shop accordingly. For example red cabbage as an accompaniment to roast beef would please the older kids but would elicit at least three "yucks" from the little ones. In other words my shopping and cooking were tailored to individual palates.

One day I came into the house with the first of many armsful of shopping bags. Happy with a job well done, I was about to return to the garage for more of the same when Bernard demanded to know, "Therese, why does it take you so long to shop?"

"I don't know. I don't think much about time, only why I'm there in the store. I compare prices, look at new items, things that are on sale, about what food combinations would taste good together. To me shopping is more than picking up groceries. There are strategies at work here!" I finished as I headed for the garage. I shook my head as I reached for more brown bags and thought, who the hell cares how long shopping takes?

Apparently, at least one person did, because the inquisition continued.

"I'm serious about this. How could it take you nearly two hours to shop? I can do it one hour tops," he pushed.

"What's the difference? I'm home now. Excuse me, there are more bags in the car," I said, slipping by him.

"Jeez, talk about a federal case!" I exhaled in the garage.

"Why did you shop at Waldbaum's today when the A&P is closer?" he asked.

"I like their deli section better, especially the liverwurst that Thérèse likes. It's worth the trip."

"Two hours is still a long time, even going to Waldbaum's. I just don't get it!" he continued.

Maybe humor?

"Look at me," I invited. "I stopped for a manicure on the way!" as I held up ten needy fingernails for inspection.

His look told me he wasn't amused.

Exasperated, frustrated and aggravated at being interrogated, I confessed.

"People talk to me in the store. I look like everyone's mother, sister or aunt," I conceded.

"What do you mean they talk to you? About what?" he demanded.

"Everything," I said.

"Like what?"

"At times, it's just 'hello,' or 'nice day.' Today, a woman asked me about wheat germ. I told her she could get more from capsules than a sprinkle of grains on cereal. She was glad to know that, thanked me and put the jar back on the shelf."

"That wasn't any of your business!" he said.

"Well, she asked my opinion. What am I supposed to do?"

"Don't answer her."

"How could I do that? A woman asks me a question. I walk by without responding? I couldn't do that. It's totally rude," I said.

"Well, no wonder it takes so long for you to shop."

"I am a citizen of the world!" I said gratefully as I put away the rest of the groceries.

Wallersee

We arrived in lovely, inviting Salzburg intending to stay for a few days, but a Mozart festival had left not a room available.

"Not even if you were president of the United States!" we were advised. No room, but at least we had been placed in good company.

There were no vacancies in any town near Salzburg. We sang and drove. Suddenly a scream from the second seat brought the van to a screeching halt. Liz had fallen against the open ashtray and cut her arm. A little first aid did the trick until we happened upon a beautiful building set on the shore of a clear lake. Sailboats were everywhere, a little reminder of sailing on my majestic Hudson River with Bernard in the sailboat he had built.

As we drove the long, flowered approach to a chateau, slowly, slowly with one eye on the sailboats, I recalled the building of his boat.

In 1947, we had been seriously dating. One night after dinner in Manhattan, I excused myself for a quick check of my makeup.

"Back in a minute!" I assured him.

I found a woman crying in the ladies room. She poured her heart out. I listened to her story. Soon, she felt better, and so did I.

Bernard, however, did not feel better at all. He had left the table, paid the check and was standing at the bar looking terribly uncomfortable.

"I'm sorry," I started.

"The next time you're going to be in the ladies room for ten minutes, let me know. I'll have another cup of coffee," he said sharply.

Outside of an occasional beer, he wasn't much of a drinker. He didn't enjoy standing at the bar. I didn't appreciate his tone of voice and overreaction. The trip home was very quiet. Before going to bed, I dashed off a Dear John letter.

He called, incredulous, when he received it. Could he come to my house with a gift he had ordered weeks ago?

No need for a gift or a visit, I wasn't interested in seeing anyone who had raised his voice to me, period!

We didn't talk for a year and a half; the "gift" had been an engagement ring.

A workaholic, he quit his job, built a sailboat, went to Florida to become a beach bum with a few friends. Probably not a bad idea since all of them had recently been on other, less-friendly beaches in the South Pacific and at places such as Anzio. This was their well-deserved rest and recreation, several years overdue.

Back to reality, in Austria, we spilled out of the van at what appeared to be a resort for American G.I.s. Everyone wanted to know if we could stay there, go sailing, swimming, play tennis. "You know, Mom, do *normal* things."

"It's gorgeous! I'd love to stay here. Let's go inside and check it out," I said.

"Do you have any vacancies?" I asked a sullen man with a thick accent.

"You *cannot* stay here!" he announced, rather pleased with himself. "This is only for the military!"

"Okay, is there someone who could look at my little girl's arm? Is there a medic here?" I almost whispered, when I wanted to shout: "Listen, buddy, I help to pay your salary! Back off!"

"You will wait *here!*" he ordered.

I winked at the kids to reassure them. His *achtung* attitude had intimidated them momentarily.

A young G.I. smiled a broad welcome as though we were "folks from home." He looked at Liz's injury, spoke gently to her as he applied a butterfly, no stitches necessary.

We chatted a bit. I thanked him, expressed regret at our not being able to stay at this spectacular resort. What a sweet child!

He thought for a moment. He came up with a possibility. He could say we were the wife and family of an officer, here to surprise him. I smiled at his naïveté, as I entertained for a split second such a delicious encounter.

"Is there an unmarried officer stationed here?" I asked.

"Yes. There's a major who's stationed here, but he's out at the moment. He'll be back in an hour or so. We could say you're *his* family. It could work. Let's try it," he coaxed.

Blessed with a flair for the dramatic, I salivated at the scene that could have played out in an Austrian Eden.

Enter "achtung."

"You cannot stay here!" he repeated.

Now I was truly interested in meeting the major, not solely for the hilarious reaction to his first encounter with his family, but to show "achtung" he shouldn't make such sweeping statements.

"We can't stay here? Just *watch* us!" I thought.

I assumed that he of the sullen countenance would have blown our cover before we had a chance to pull it off. It had been a delightful thought! What a scene might have ensued: "What do you mean you have no wife? Darling, what has happened to you? You're here for R&R; you've been physically and mentally exhausted, but have you also lost your memory? Surely you remember Anne, Joseph, Mary, Edward, Christine, Elizabeth, Thérèse, Peter and John!"

I still regret a missed opportunity.

That plan scrapped, the young medic was not about to give up. The thought of spending his leisure hours with numerous kids from home intrigued him, I'm sure.

"I have an idea. I'll say you're *my* wife. That would work."

I laughed and asked his age.

"I'm twenty-two," he said, chest fully expanded.

"I appreciate your thought, but I'm old enough to be your mother. Thanks for everything. We'll keep driving. We'll find something. I'm happy you're stationed in such a paradise," I said as I shook his hand and gave him a maternal kiss on the cheek.

"Achtung" was nowhere to be seen as we left, most likely off haunting another part of the resort.

We stopped to eat while we drank in the beauty of Austria, then drove on, convinced we'd have to sleep in the car since lodging had eluded us in town after town.

Now it was dark and unsettling. I don't know how long we were on the road or what the hour was. I judged that I had heard, *Wouldn't It Be Loverly* from *My Fair Lady* for at least an hour.

"All I want is a room somewhere,
Far away from the cold night air,
With one e-nooooormous chair,
Ow, wouldn't it be loverly?"

Now the tired little voices sang wearily, lyrics interspersed with yawns.

Then, around a bend, it appeared: A sign bearing that long awaited word — VACANCIES. Yea team!

We pulled into a large, dimly lit parking area. We sat for a moment, then Joseph hopped out to inquire about rooms for the ten of us. He returned looking very pleased, accompanied by a smiling gent who had come for our luggage.

At the front desk, a lovely lady greeted us with, "You look tired."

"Yes," I agreed. "I am a bit tired."

"Certainly with all these children, you must have some clothes that need laundering?" she asked.

"How'd you know?" I joked.

"If your son will show Will where they are, he'll take them to the laundry room. We will deliver it to your room in the morning," she smiled.

"Wonderful!" I giggled. "Wonderful!"

"Wunderbar!" she instructed me as I climbed the stairs to our rooms.

"Wunderbar!" I echoed.

The kids were already choosing rooms without much discussion when I reached the second floor. They were a tired bunch.

"Brush your teeth. Say your prayers and into bed!" I called.

"Could we just sleep in our underwear for tonight?" someone asked.

"Sure!" I wearily answered. "That'll be fine!"

I would have agreed to hopping into bed shoes and all had they asked. I was that tired.

"Goodnight and God bless, Mommy," rang the chorus.

"Goodnight and God bless," I answered.

A sparkling, knotty pine room, colorful quilts on each bed and the laundry's being done while we sleep. Heaven!

What seemed like twenty minutes later was actually the next morning, everyone arrived in my room to share a spectacular treat.

"Look Mommy, a lake! Come out on the balcony and see," Liz chirped.

"Balcony? Lake?" I repeated. The best a *non-morning* person could muster.

Sure enough, French windows opened onto a delightful little balcony overlooking a lake.

"Could we go swimming, Mom?" almost everyone asked.

"Of course," I yawned.

"Now? Could we go now?" the same group pushed.

"What time is it, anyway?" I asked.

"It's seven o'clock!" Chris said.

"Oh no!" I rebelled. "Seven a.m.! Why are you up so early? We went to bed late last night. I thought you'd sleep in this morning. The air is cold this early in the mountains," I stumbled.

"Do you mean this early in the morning?" some wise guy wanted to know.

I punched my pillow, dropped into it as a hint. That worked for a good minute and a half.

"All right, all right. I'll get up now. Someone check *very* quietly to see if there's anyone in the dining room. I hope they *have* a dining room. I didn't ask last night. I was more interested in bed than breakfast."

The messengers arrived to announce that there was a small area where people were having breakfast.

"They were eating sausages, pancakes … ," they drooled. "They even have maple syrup!"

"Wow! Even maple syrup! What a place!" I joked. "Notice any coffee? By the way, is the dining room so small that we should go down a few at a time?"

"No, but I think we'll have to sit at a few tables. There are no big tables at all," Ed advised.

I followed the kids down the stairs. They wondered why I laughed out loud as I passed a hall table.

There, on the table, was an Austrian magazine with a photo of the Pope on the cover. The caption read, "Papa nix der pill!" Sometimes one doesn't need to know the language. I don't know how many guests had noticed the blaring announcement in print as they passed. I was very conscious of the strange juxtaposition of our entry into the dining room so shortly after reading Papa's pronouncement. It was a polite room, not even a snicker.

There was a dog in residence, perhaps a cocker spaniel, whose name was Schvenny. She/he/it had a rock nearby at all times. Fascinated by the rock, it would carry it from place to place, drop it directly in front of its face and stare. Somehow, the animal never tired of looking at the rock from all angles.

We never tired of watching the dog watch the rock. A fellow guest, from God knows where, joined in the rock watch, looked in my direction and asked, "Philosophe?"

I agreed. Schvenny was "pondering the notion of rockness."

For a moment, I was transported back to philosophy class where such things were often "pondered." Living a bound-to-the-earth sort of life at that time, I often wished I were home, in the kitchen flipping pancakes, cooking a roast or baking a torte — those things I understood. Not much time for pondering, just keep on truckin', whipping out meals, laundry and term papers.

Now I had time to ponder: A leisurely trip through Europe with no itinerary, free of domestic chores.

Yes, I could have joined Schvenny in his pondering. I've done foolish things along the way, was never audience-shy, but lying on my tummy next to a dog analyzing a rock while visiting a foreign country was going to have to wait.

The swimming question came up again.

"Yes, we'll all go swimming. Get your suits on, wear sandals and don't forget towels. We'll get ready, go down to the lake, but wait a while before diving in. We've just eaten a big breakfast," I said as my eye caught sight of several stacks of freshly laundered clothes on the dresser. They were not only washed, but they were also ironed to perfection, even underwear! I thought of messing them up a little so the kids didn't get the false notion this would continue stateside. I joined them in luxuriating with each change of clothes.

Soon our kids were indistinguishable from kids of many nations who also called Wallersee home for a few days. I love that about children: "hail fellow, well met" all the way. No strange, awkward newness when they meet; they became instant friends. It's beautiful. I believe some of my kids take it a step further, picking up accents of one and all acquaintances. Within seven minutes, I heard Chris call to her new little English friend, "Shall I tip you ovah?" as they tubed around the lake.

Why several adopted accents, I don't know. Was it a matter of "When in Rome, do as the Romans do"? Who knows? In any case, it worked while in the company of strangers. And it was great fun. Siblings, however, are inclined to take a dim view of such shenanigans; nearly forty years after the fact, at family gatherings, "Shall I tip you ovah?" still surfaces.

Always over the evening meal there were lively, interesting updates of the day's doings.

"Did you see the father of the English girl I met?" Chris asked.

"Oh, you mean the one you sound just like now?" Mary wondered.

"That's enough, Mary. Yes, Chris I saw her father. Why?" I encouraged.

"Well, when they came to the dock, her father took off his pants," Chris said.

"Well, you didn't expect him to dive in with his pants on, did you?" Ed asked.

"No I didn't, but that's not *all* he took off!" she announced.

"What do you mean?" I asked, not sure I wanted to hear the answer.

Everyone waited.

"He took off his *leg*!" Chris said.

"You're nuts! How could anyone take off his *leg*?" Mary demanded to know.

"He had a wooden leg, well it wasn't wooden, but anyway it wasn't *his*," Chris said.

"Well if it wasn't his, whose was it?" Edward asked.

"It was in *his* pants," Joe joined the conversation, "so it had to be his."

"It was his," Chris assured us.

133

"You said it wasn't his," Edward added. "Make up your mind!"

"Did he pay for it?" I asked.

"Yes!" Chris insisted.

"Then it was *his*!" I ended the intrigue.

"I meant it wasn't the one he was *born* with," Chris explained. "He lost his leg in the war."

"That's a shame. It happened to a lot of men, but he apparently hasn't let it stand in his way," I said.

"It couldn't stand because … ," Ed started.

"That's not funny," Chris chided.

I agreed.

Back from the lake, we walked around the lush grounds. Behind the motel, in pristine whitewashed buildings, sang a group of gleeful employees, washing, ironing and laughing. "Felicity" is the word Austrians have adopted as their own to describe the overriding emotion Austrian people as a whole exude. The joyous launderers exemplified the fact.

Our last breakfast there was notable since Schvenny was not in sight.

"Where's Schvenny?" inquired Joseph.

"He's not himself this morning. We don't know why. He's acting strange," the hostess answered.

"Uh-oh" murmured Edward, exchanging a knowing glance with Mary.

"What do you mean, Ed?" I asked. "Do you know what happened to Schvenny?"

"Not really. It's just that … ," he hesitated.

"Just what?"

"Well, last night Mary and I came into the dining room to watch him watch the rock," he started.

"And then what happened?" I asked.

134

"Well, I had a piece of fishing line … ," he said.

"Yeah, then what did you do with the fishing line?" I said softly, in order not to frighten off the big one I was trying to reel in.

"It wasn't anything bad, Mom," Mary assured me.

"So, if it wasn't anything bad, just tell me what happened next," I said.

"Ed, tell Mommy," Ed's partner in crime encouraged him.

"I tied the fishing line around the rock a few times," he started reluctantly. Another glance shot toward Mary, both broke down in helpless laughter, the type usually reserved for church or other solemn locations.

Words were now out of the question. Tears streamed down the faces of the two suspects. Without knowing why, we soon all joined in their contagious eruptions.

Finally, Ed blinked back the last few tears, sniffed once or twice and told all.

"Okay, after I wrapped the fishing line around the rock, I held the end of the line and sat at a table. I tugged *very* gently on the line. Schvenny looked at the moving rock, then looked at us like he was asking us, "Did you see that?" so I pulled it a little more. First he followed it only with his eyes, but stayed in the same spot."

"That's right," Mary agreed "but then …" laughter rendered the two wordless once more.

We waited. Mary recovered first.

"It was weird. Ed moved the rock about a foot away. The dog jumped up in the air, a strange jump, chased his tail, jumped that funny jump again and wagged his tail. All the while he made this funny little sound, not a bark or a growl, kinda yippy. I think he was happy!"

"Delirious, I'm sure!" I observed. "So, what did you do then?"

"I unwrapped the rock, picked up my line and left," Ed answered.

"Schvenny was still celebrating when we left," Mary added.

"Celebrating?" I asked.

"Yeah. We think all these years he was trying to make the rock move by staring at it. Ed just helped his dream come true. That's why he acted so, so, uh …"

"Happy!" Ed put a quick end to the story.

We reluctantly left Wallersee, where we had been involved in "normal" activities not "stupid" pastimes such as touring Europe for nine weeks.

"You boys remind me of a story I once heard of another boy who complained about traveling with his mother."

"Who was he?" Edward asked.

"I don't know his name, only that he, too, complained about a trip abroad," I coaxed.

"So what does that have to do with us?" Joe joined in.

"You two complain and so did the boy in the story," I said.

"What did his mother do? Did she make him go to Europe?" Edward wondered.

"I think she was determined that Europe would be their destination. I heard only the beginning of the story, where her son complained," I said.

"You're always telling us travel is educational, we're lucky and we should enjoy it. Is that what *his* mother said?" Joseph finally asked.

"Not exactly. He said, 'Mother, I don't want to go to Europe.' His mother said, 'Shut up and keep swimming!'"

Two nasal snort-like sounds were the only reactions followed by a delightful silence that lasted at least two miles.

"Mommy," Liz began. "In Ireland, John told you where to turn. Then someone else told you to turn left in another country. Could I tell you which way to turn next time you don't know?"

"Sure you may, in a while. At the moment I'm heading toward the highway ... I think. I'll let you know."

"I told you to turn right in Ireland, remember Mommy?" John beamed.

"I remember, John. That was a big help," I said.

"Remember when you said we could vote on which way to turn once?" Mary asked.

"I remember it well. It was the only time you all agreed on something this whole trip. You told me to turn left. I did and later found out we missed a war being waged in Bratislava ten miles to the right. *That* left turn was a great idea!"

"Well didn't you *know* there was a war going on in that country?" Anne asked.

"How could I have known that?" I asked in my defense. "I've never even *heard* of Bratislava, much less what goes on there. Anyway, wouldn't you think we'd have heard war noises from a mere ten miles away?"

"What are war noises, Mommy?" Peter asked.

"Bombs, hand grenades, rifles, you know, all the things people of one country use to kill people in another country," illuminated Mary, our war correspondent of the hour.

"Why do people kill each other?" Peter asked, adding, "That isn't very nice!"

"You're right, sweetheart. That *isn't* very nice," I said.

"Then why do they do it?" Peter persisted.

"I don't know. When I was a little girl and heard about war for the first time, I had a good idea," I said.

"What was your idea?" Thérèse asked.

"If leaders of two countries disagreed about something, the two of them should fight it out and leave everyone else alone!"

"You should tell somebody," Edward suggested. "That's a good idea!"

"No one would listen, Edward. Usually groups of *old* men decide to send most of the *young* men to war. If mothers were in power, there would be *no* war," I assured him.

"'Cause mommies are kind?" Peter asked.

"Because they carry life within their bodies until that life can live on its own in the world. They don't want anyone hurting that little life regardless of how tall he's grown," I answered.

"'Cause Mommies are kind!" Peter declared.

"I think most mommies are kind and love their children too much to have them killed in war. War doesn't come from kindness and love. I think it's just a game men play when they become leaders of countries."

"There's the highway, Mommy," Liz observed. "Turn left 'cause maybe there's a war on the right again!"

"Okay, left turn it is. Austria is a beautiful country. Just sit back for a while. Look at the mountains and lakes. Let's be *really* quiet while we drive and think about all the kind, happy people we've met."

"And one happy dog!" Ed added.

Mary elbowed Ed in the ribs to remind him that subject was closed.

"I liked Schvenny," Chris said. "What do you think he'll do when he finds out he can't move his rock again by staring at it?"

"He'll be depressed and his owners will take him to see Doctor Sigmund Von Poodle, dog psychiatrist in Vienna," Anne laughed.

"But there will be a problem when Doctor Von Poodle tells him to lie on the couch," Joseph announced.

"Why?" Thérèse asked, a perfect straight man.
"He's not allowed on the furniture!"

Two Naughty Boys

"How are my two baby loves?"
I asked as I sat between Peter and John on the sofa.

Giggles were the only response.

"How are the two most *precious* boys in the whole world?" I asked as I tickled their tummies and nuzzled their freshly shampooed heads.

Belly laughs this time.

"Mommy's going to tell you a story. How do all good stories begin?"

"I know," said Peter, "Once upon a time."

"Yep, once upon a time," echoed John.

"That's right," I smiled.

"Once upon a time, there were three bears: a Mama bear ... ,"

140

"A Papa bear," Peter added quickly, his bright blue eyes dancing.

"And a littoo baby baow," finished John, squeezing his shoulders together, taking on the role of the baby bear, as he made himself as tiny as possible.

"The bears lived in a lovely little cottage in the woods. It was a sparkly clean, white house with yellow window boxes and shutters. The shutters had honey pot shapes carved in them because … ,"

"Bears love honey!" Peter offered, shoulders proudly back.

John nodded in agreement and added, "Yep, baows love honey."

"What kind of flowers do the bears have in their window boxes?" I asked.

"Our window boxes have red and white flowers," Peter announced.

"Yep, wed and white," John agreed once again, regarding his "big" brother, thirteen months his senior, with a "how do you know all this stuff?" look.

"The three bears went for a little walk," I started.

"That's when a little girl named Goldilocks knocked at the door," Peter added.

"But nobody was home," John chimed in.

"That's right. When Goldilocks didn't get an answer to her knock, she walked into the house of the three bears."

"That wasn't a good thing to do," Peter remarked.

"It was naughty," John said.

"That's right," I agreed.

The story continued in the oral tradition of oft-told stories, the book used only for picture references as the tale unfolded.

With the bears finally settled back in their house, the visit from Goldilocks history, moral discovered, a glance at the clock ended story time.

"I've got to set my hair now, so think about your lunch and Daddy's breakfast. I'll be back upstairs in a few minutes. Please play quietly for now; Daddy is still sleeping. Your books are on the hearth along with the walking Mickey Mouse and Donald Duck Uncle Joe bought you. Have them walk down this plank," I suggested. "Good thing the hearth is raised. We'll place one end of the plank on the hearth and the other end on the rug, see? Nice and quiet. Okay? Good boys. I'll be up in a few minutes."

Sitting on the braided rug, our angels played quietly, quietly. How blessed our lives have been by their arrivals.

Perfect time for a quick shampoo and set. Shampoo finished, I listen at the foot of the five stairs that led to the living floor. I could hear bits of conversation and laughter from the two soul mates. Tiptoe back to the bathroom where a dozen rollers were quickly applied. Great, everything is still quiet as I climb the few stairs. Not completely silent, though. I couldn't quite identify the muffled sounds emanating from the dining room.

If there were words, they were badly garbled, accompanied by a moaning noise. It was spooky. *My* words were very clear: "My God! What happened here?" I asked as I crunched through wall-to-wall cereal; the deep, rich multi-colored braided carpets were now a Special K beige and Raisin Bran brown. Certainly this was not the work of two angels I had so recently tickled! John sat on the sofa reading a book. He couldn't possibly look up to meet my glance; he was really into the book, which happened to be upside down. The heaving of his chest suggested recent marathon running.

In the dining room, a stereo sat on the floor for their use. There knelt Peter, smiling, humming as he held a stick of butter to a

Mario Lanza record as it turned. Two cereal boxes were in evidence. I didn't check for prints.

I would have loved to have witnessed the run-up to this scene, most likely a little dance to several tunes. Someone, deciding the dance lacked something, added cereal for texture underfoot, plus a stick of butter to the record for a change of tempo. There, that was better.

"I can't believe two good little boys would ever," I said in disbelief.

Their cleanup, one flake at a time was painfully slow. All their energy had been spent on quick and quiet mayhem. I watched for a while, then told them to go their room to think about their naughtiness. Downcast, they marched down the steps to repent, I assumed.

I swept up the topsoil, would vacuum later when I could make noise without disturbing anyone. Mario Lanza was freed of his butter bath after about forty-five minutes of effort. I rejoiced as I walked down to check on the penitents.

When I reached the second stair, I saw the two dashing madly between the pink tiled bathroom, over the white marble threshold to the doorway of the finished basement. They emptied two small green buckets of water down the carpeted stairs, the last in a series, judging by the squishy sounds my shoes made. A retrieval of the buckets, a swat on the behind of each culprit and a strong wish for a wet/dry vacuum followed the discovery in rapid succession. The hall was only slightly damp. Old towels stomped on the cellar stairs got rid of most of the water.

Our bedroom door opened. Peter called across the hall from their bedroom, "Hi, Daddy. We were quiet so you could sleep!"

"Yeah, quiet!" echoed John.

"Thank you." He asked, "What have you fellows been up to?"

Before they could answer, incriminating themselves, I asked what he'd like for breakfast. We all went up to the kitchen together. The two climbed on the bench against the brick wall, waiting for lunch, which by rights should have been bread and water. The three men ate, one ate breakfast and two ate lunch.

The funniest line of the day came from Bernard.

"Aren't they wonderful? They were so quiet I slept much later than usual. So, did you get much studying done? You should take advantage of these quiet mornings."

"You're right," I agreed as I cleared the table. "I devoted this morning to a case study."

"Really? What's it about?"

"It deals with the degree of frustration an individual is able to tolerate before going stark, raving mad."

"That sounds morose."

"Depends upon the cast of characters. More coffee?"

Kindberg

While we traveled, we were never bored.

The older kids looked at maps, travel books and compared souvenirs, each complimenting herself or himself on exquisite taste. As we drove we sang our favorite show tunes, many from shows in which some of the passengers had appeared in the not-too-distant past at the Presbyterian Church in Palisades.

Just like the rest of the trip, singing was never planned. It sort of erupted. Lifting one's voice in song can be very therapeutic, a wonderful tension breaker and a great outlet for the poison called sibling rivalry.

When Chris broke out in, *"You coax the blues right out of the horn, Mame. You charm the husk right off a' the corn, Mame,"* as she had sung it for Monsignor Johnson's twenty-fifth anniversary revue, Mary tutted and asked, "Do we have to sing that dumb song *again*? She only likes to sing it so everyone will say how cute she looked on stage with your mink scarf and those ruffled pink pajamas. That's the only reason, Mommy, she probably doesn't even *like* the dumb song."

Singing is akin to meditation for me. And the enemy — the kids — knew it. Nothing interrupts a song already begun, so I continued to sing,

"You've got those banjoes strummin'
And plunkin' out a tune to beat the band,
The whole plantation's hummin'
Since you brought Dixie back to Dixieland."

From the second seat came protestations from Chris, something to the effect that she would never sing a song she considered dumb and, "Anyway, I sang a solo which is more than *you* ever did."

I squeezed in a quick, "Girls, please," and continued with,
"You made the cotton easy to pick, Mame,
You give my old mint julep a kick, Mame."

"I guess you don't remember, Miss Movie Star," Mary continued, "but after that line you winked and kicked and everyone could see that rubber band that held on your evening slippers. Didn't you hear them laugh?"

"Yes, I heard them laugh. I made them laugh when I winked and kicked so high just like a Rockette," Chris said.

146

"You mean a rocket, don't you? You know, flat all round with a pointy head?" Mary answered.

Chris cried, "Mom, make her stop!"

That cry signaled victory for Mary, at least for this round, and I finished solo:

"*You made the old magnolia tree*
Blossom at the mention of your name,
You made us feel alive again,
You've given us the drive again,
To make the South revive again, Mame."

We rounded a corner and drove into a mini wonderland, Kindberg, Austria. Street lights were adorned with hand-carved wooden figures and the village green was filled with a merry band of men in lederhosen and Tyrolean hats, all doing their own thing in an oompah band. How could we pass through such enchantment?

I quickly parked the bus and we all joined in the knee-slapping, swaying and abundant joy which so marked the Austrians we had the pleasure of meeting.

We stayed in Kindberg for several days, improving the economy considerably since the shops were as captivating as the natives. An occasional glance even today at the little gold frame that holds Edelweiss brings a torrent of memories of Kindberg, one of which I would gladly erase.

Each morning as we entered the dining room, the waitress would greet us warmly. We attempted the same. Thank goodness smiles are universal. We did a *lot* of smiling. I sensed very strongly that the woman who served us so graciously wanted to know all about us, but she had to settle for clever retorts from me such as holding up the appropriate number of fingers to tell ages as she pointed to each child.

A retired American lived at the hotel. I'm sure he asked questions at her request. Her interest in us and her kindness grew with each day and ended in tears on the morning of our departure. Her tears flowed from a fountain of love; mine, as I'll explain, from humiliation.

As we were about to leave, she poured another cup of coffee for me and brought out a special little pastry. I thanked her by body language one more time, licking my lips and rubbing my tummy, as any *child* would do. She smiled and to my surprise sat down and we toasted each other with coffee.

Our mutual friend, the interpreter, asked questions for her. First, where was my husband? When I answered that he had died the previous year, she shook her head in disbelief and tears rolled down her cheeks. Nothing should end on such a somber note, so I told her that my late husband was half-Austrian. She smiled and nodded her head approvingly. There. That was better. She then assured me through the friendly gent that most of my children looked Austrian. She added that she had come from a large family and our stay there had made her feel at home again. I smiled and added that her hospitality had made us feel like part of her family.

Enter Joe, who informed me that the luggage was strapped to the bus roof and the natives were getting restless. He asked for a shilling to buy Wash and Dries from a machine in the men's room. Good thought! We kept a good supply in the glove compartment and their use, along with a quick brush of everyone's hair, altered the picture of "ugly Americans" before we checked into restaurants or hotels. Joe returned from the men's room and I put my hand out for the purchase.

"I'll hold them till we get to the car," Joe said.

From the happy exchange of family facts and the special coffee and cake with which I had been honored I felt special and a little playful. I reached out to grab the container from his hand.

"I paid for them, I'll hold them. Now hand them over!" I insisted.

The formerly happy, kind waitress jumped up from the table and cleared away the dishes in a frenzy, glaring at me and shaking her head in disbelief. The interpreter stopped interpreting, shook his head and sat there in disbelief.

"What a mercurial group," I thought. I was stunned and directed my gaze to the little packet and wondered how anyone could have squeezed three towelettes into such a small container.

I could no longer bear the sudden mood swing and so I addressed the waitress. Pointing to the purchase I gestured that I always use these on the children's hands and faces when we stop for meals. Of course the words were accompanied by the usual gestures of washing hands and circles on both cheeks. Now glances and words were exchanged among the waitress, interpreter and several other men who also lived there.

As I opened the container — which held condoms, not towelettes — I gasped and, through clenched, teeth told Joe they weren't towelettes and chances were good that I would kill him before we reached the car. That evening when Joe and I discussed the "purchase," he asked, "Why did you give me the money if you knew what kind of machines they have in men's rooms? Don't they have them in men's rooms in America?"

I remained calm and assured him that, although I was attempting to be both mother and father, I had no intention of frequenting the men's room at home or abroad.

A friend later suggested that after our hasty retreat, the Austrians had a good laugh at remembering a crazy American woman who demonstrated the use to which she put the contents of the surprise package. And more than once I have thought they could have drawn an analogy between me and the "old woman who lived in a shoe. She had so many children, she didn't know what to do," … evidently!

Bad Day

Wonderful feelings of gratitude filled me on the two-and-a-half-mile ride home from school. How blessed I felt to have this opportunity to finish college, taught by bright, dedicated professors who viewed the role of teacher as vocation, not simply a job.

My revered professors, mainly Dominican Sisters of Sparkill, New York, made education exciting. What an art! I shall be eternally grateful not only for a great education but for the privilege of spending three years in the company of quality humans who knew the world and could have been well-compensated *in* the world for their talents but chose to follow Him.

I drove up Oak Tree Road happily anticipating my conversation with Bernard, sharing the gems of learning I had been offered in psych class in the preceding hour.

"I'm home! Where is everyone?" I sang as I charged into the house.

"Shhh, Mommy," Liz, our number six, whispered. "Daddy didn't feel very well so we brushed his hair and put cold cloths on his head and hands, then he fell asleep. He's on the sofa in the living room."

But an hour and a half ago he was fine, I thought. Just before I left he had danced me around the kitchen as "I'll Be Seeing You," *the* song of WWII years, played on the kitchen radio. I had assumed my return would be as pleasant.

150

"All right, dear," I whispered in return. "That was very sweet of you to take such good care of Daddy. Thank you for that."

"Oh, it wasn't just me," she started.

"It wasn't just I, Liz," I corrected.

"You weren't here at *all*!" she answered. We dropped the subject when Bernard chided me from the other room for encouraging grammatical perfection one more time.

"I swear, Therese, if you saw someone drowning and he yelled, "You *ain't* goin' in the right direction," you'd cringe, correct him, *then* save him … in that order!"

I smiled in agreement as I bent to kiss him hello, then proceeded to gather wet washcloths.

"Bad day?" I needlessly asked. "Did that last dance do you in?"

He was ashen.

"I felt weak after you left, told the kids to start their homework. The girls insisted on making me feel better with your coldcloth treatment."

"It makes *them* feel as though they're helping, like I feel when I kiss them and make them all better whatever the ailment. A kiss or a cold cloth works wonders on little bumps and bruises," I smiled.

"There are some things that *can't* be fixed with a cold cloth," Bernard sighed.

I nodded.

"Or a kiss," I thought as I walked downstairs to our bedroom, calling back to him that I'd be up shortly to start dinner.

"No hurry," he said. "I think I'll go back to sleep. Take your time."

On my way downstairs his words echoed in my head: "Some things can't be fixed with a cold cloth." I closed the bedroom door, threw myself across the bed, finally surrendering to the truth in his statement. I wept without restraint, not a luxury I'd afforded myself prior to this.

"Oh God," I sobbed. "Please help him. Please be with us. There's nothing *I* can do to help him. Nothing! I feel so helpless, so hopeless. I know I have to be strong, but I'm *not* strong. How long can I smile and pretend everything's fine when I see him slowly dying day by day, a little at a time. I wonder if he knows. …"

"Mommy," Chris called as she approached the locked bedroom door. "Are you in there?"

"Uh-huh," I answered.

"Are you going to stay in there?" she wondered.

"Uh-uh," I said.

I cleared my throat, while trying to clear my mind.

"I'm changing my clothes, honey. I'll be upstairs in a minute," I stalled.

While she climbed the few stairs, I slipped into the bathroom, splashed cold water around my eyes and added a touch of lipstick preparing myself for center stage one more time. My audience of ten would soon again be watching every gesture, reading each facial expression in order to gauge the emotional health of the family. If Mommy is serene all is well. No understudy for *this* role. No sick days or personal days off for recouping. The show must go on and I *am* the show. This little world of my making depends upon me for a stellar performance at each and every appearance.

When I walked into the kitchen, Chris asked, "Where are you going?" bringing an instant smile to my face and heart as well. Lipstick indicated some activity *outside* the house for the most part. The sight of lipstick on me sometimes sent the kids running to the garage to be first into the car.

"I'm not going anywhere but here to my cozy kitchen," I reassured her.

"What are we having for dinner?" she asked.

"Close your eyes and what do you see?" I teased.

"Mommy! Really what are we having?" she insisted.

"Steak, mashed potatoes, string beans, salad and a big glass of milk!" I told her.

"Some girls in my class are wearing stockings," Mary announced. "Not to school, but other times."

"Do you like that idea?" I asked.

She shrugged and said, "I guess it's okay."

"Why do you think girls like wearing stockings instead of anklets or knee socks?" I asked.

"Makes 'em feel grown-up," she answered.

"That's right. Girls are little girls for a short time. Then they're grown-up for the rest of their lives. Why rush it?" I said.

"I don't want to wear stockings … yet!" she ended the conversation as she ran out into the front yard. "Ed, toss me the ball!"

Anne walked into the kitchen.

"Daddy wants a cup of coffee," she announced. As she took milk from the fridge she asked, "No sugar, right?"

"That's right. No sugar."

Dinner on the stove, I sat at the kitchen table, leafing through the Rockland County edition of *The Bergen Evening Record*. I needed this time before I could be involved in pleasant, casual conversation, a shifting of gears.

"Anne, want to call the troops? Dinner's almost ready," I said.

Bernard walked to the front door, whistled and watched as Kramer Kids came running from all directions.

"Wash your hands before you sit down," he said.

He was stronger after a rest, smiling as he sat at the table and cheerfully asked, "So, how was school today?" Quick responses came in turn from each of the children as the pre-schoolers, innocent eyes aglow, drank in all the exciting news about this wondrous place called school. The atmosphere had changed from somber to joyous in less than an hour. While I served dinner, my face reflected the healing joy with which children bless us, but my heart still rode a roller coaster of emotions.

Was the opening of the floodgates a short time ago a simple "giving in," releasing an emotional safety valve or a necessary preparatory step, a lock-like lowering of my heart and spirit to a deeper level of awareness and of grief?

Evening chores behind me, I read for a few hours trying to make sense of "ponderings" of various philosophers. My "ponderings" were terribly mundane. Did I take that last load of laundry out of the dryer? Did I sign *every* paper that everyone had brought home from school? Did I remember to make Mary's peanut butter sandwich on whole wheat minus jelly? (That luncheon choice still dries the roof of my mouth!)

Shortly after midnight, I slid quietly into bed. Automatically his arm reached out, drawing me to him. He was fast asleep. I reluctantly listened to his heartbeat as I rested on his chest and wept.

I didn't want to hear his heart beat. Not tonight. I wanted to bolt from this one place of rest where I had felt most secure. I ached to hear ... a strong ... steady ... beat ... that didn't plan on stopping anytime soon. If that were not to be, I wanted to be excused from listening to the *countdown*. I shook my head in disbelief as the discordant rhythm of his failing heart now had lyrics, "in ... sickness ... and in ... health. ..."

"Therese?" he murmured.

"I'm here, honey," I whispered through a torrent of tears.

"Until ... death ... do you ... part," continued the rhythmic reminder.

BAD DAY

I patted his right forearm in reassurance, raised my head to kiss his cheek, gently lulling him back to sleep with, "Shh. Everything is fine. I'm here. I'm right here."

Italy

Not much surfaces in my memory of Italy.

I know, I know. The grandeur of Rome, the romance of Venice, etc. Our stay was brief. I scare easily. Our retreat was hasty. Two things stand out.

Stopping at a restaurant for our evening meal just before the rain started. An hour or so later, we left the table and started for the door when the lights went out. Chris, not quite ten years old, screamed and laughed at the same time, "Someone pinched me! Someone pinched me!"

Well there's *one* wish come true. I had the children; I don't explain them.

At the door of the restaurant, a policeman opened an umbrella and offered to walk me to the car. I thanked him and explained I was not alone. He said he realized the children were mine and asked how many there were. When I said there were nine, he asked, "Would you like to try for ten?" I declined the offer. He escorted us to the bus nevertheless.

As we drove along the highway, the van's low beams died. I used high beams, which wasn't bad on a divided highway, at least in the beginning. After hours of motorists flashing high beams in my eyes I decided to stop at the next service station. The mechanic spoke no English. A fellow with whom he had been speaking translated my dilemma.

The mechanic at first attempted to remedy the problem from under the dashboard. I said we'd get out of the car to give him more room since he had the broadest shoulders I'd ever seen. No, he insisted, he had plenty of room, so the translator said.

I noticed perspiration running down his face and thought at one point he looked up my skirt. I chastised myself for having such a thought." Don't be ridiculous, the man is in cramped quarters, working vigorously at fixing the lights. Besides, he sees the kids. You're not 21, riding through Europe in a convertible with your hair blowing in the breeze. Wise up."

By now, three or four men had gathered outside the garage. The translator told me that the mechanic wanted to test the lights. The mechanic hopped into the driver's seat. The men laughed and said something to the driver and off we went. He switched the lights on and off to lend legitimacy to the ride. Every time he shifted he ran his hand up my leg. I moved closer to Joseph who shared the front seat but the mechanic's reach adapted accordingly. The road we traveled was the blackest imaginable, matching my mood. I wanted to deck him. He stopped the bus and got out to check the lights. I should have run him over. I told Joseph to exit along with me. I put my hand on Joe's shoulder and told him to cough until I told him to stop. He wanted to know why.

"Just pretend you're sick. Pretend you're throwing up. Anything. It's very important."

"Why, Mom? I feel fine," he said.

"Because every time this guy shifts, his hand slips off the stick shift onto my leg. If he weren't so big, I'd punch him out," I confided, maternally.

Joe laughed out loud and asked in utter disbelief. "He's doing that to *you*, Mom?"

"That isn't funny! I should have taken off and left him to walk back to the garage. When we get into the bus, you get in first and cough a lot and blow your nose and I'll console you madly. Maybe it'll remind him of his mother. At least I'll be out of reach."

Joseph emitted one little inappropriate giggle and quickly turned it into a peculiar cough when I gave him an elbow in the ribs to remind him that the "play's the thing." As we pulled up in front of the garage, the mechanic shook his head from side to side for all his friends to see. I couldn't imagine what sort of sick game they had in mind. I paid the bill, tore out of the station crying, drove for hours, passing places I had planned to visit, Venice among them.

Somehow, the thought of being at home and in charge was most appealing. I didn't enjoy the role of powerless victim imposed by the burly mechanic.

Anne slept during the alleged checking of lights.

When she woke to my sobs, she said we should have told her what he was doing, she'd have hit him over the head with her purse. I've always seen my life in headlines. This low episode would have been: "American Widow and Her Nine Children Slain by Burly Mechanic in Italy."

Thank God Anne slept.

How Do I Love You?

"I think I'll give the kitchen floor a really good scrubbing," I said.

"Why now?" Bernard asked. "Your timing is off."

"What do you mean?" I asked.

"It's just off, that's all."

"If it is off, it'll stay that way unless you explain what you mean. You repeat that once in a while."

"That's because it's true. Your timing is off," he said.

"The babies have just gone down for a nap. The older kids won't be home from school for an hour and a half. Can't think of a better time to scrub the floor. A fast scrub, a coat of wax and it'll look like new. I never tire of this pattern, brick is very forgiving of little spills," I said as I took a pail of hot sudsy water and a brush to the floor.

"*How* do you love me?" Bernard asked as he watched me scrub the floor from the dining room side of the counter.

"Talk about *timing*!" I laughed loudly and put down the brush momentarily. I asked the timing expert, "Does the view of a charwoman at her work evoke thoughts of not only love but *ways* of loving?"

"Why don't I give your question serious thought?" I said with a smile. "It deserves a much more thorough answer than I can give you now. Besides I'm a little out of breath at the moment."

"I am serious. I really want to know."

"I know you are. Let's get this straight. You know I love you. No question about *that*, is there?"

"No. I know you love me. I want to know *how* you love me. That's all."

"How do I love thee? Let me count the ways," I mumbled.

"Everything's a joke to you, isn't it?" he said, a little miffed.

"Now come on. You have to admit that most men wouldn't ask a question like that at a time like this. It's ludicrous! Frankly, I've never thought *how*."

"This is a big house for you to take care of, isn't it?" he said, looking around. "Someday, when the kids are grown and have moved away, we'll find a beautiful apartment, light and spacious."

"Beautiful apartment is an oxymoron," I said. "I love this house. We had plans for this before we had children. Besides, I'm a peasant. I need a little soil under my fingernails now and then. I

160

love the azalea garden where I plant Mother's Day gifts from you and the children, and the rose bushes that climb the south side of the house. Besides our babies will never grow up and move away. I love our life just the way it is. It's my fondest dream come true. You know that," I protested.

"And what about the yard full of dogwood trees?" I continued. "I dug each one from our woods and transplanted them to make our back yard beautiful. Apartment? Not for me!"

"I always lived in apartments," he said. "We could find one in a beautiful area. I like the convenience of apartment living. Nothing we have to think about now, but someday I'd like it."

"Drop me a card now and then, dear, my roots are deeply planted here on Swan Street."

"Well that's done," I said, dropping the brush into the water and rising to my feet. "It'll be dry in no time. Now I can write you an answer to the question of the day. 'How do I love you,' wasn't it? It won't take long. I'll be finished before naps are over. I'll wash my hands and start."

"What do you mean? You're *writing* it? Why don't you *tell* me?"

"When we speak I get lost in your eyes. It's easier for me to write," I said truthfully.

"Who writes an answer to a question like that?" he demanded to know, ignoring a great compliment.

"Only a woman with really lousy timing!" I answered and went downstairs to compose.

Ten minutes later, I found Bernard sitting in the living room, looking out across the back yard, deep in thought. Probably dreaming up more trick questions!

"Here you go," I said, handing him a piece of loose-leaf paper. "Here's your answer, well the nearest I can come to an answer anyway. How many men inspire poetry? You're *so* lucky!"

He read, smiled, shook his head as tears welled up in his eyes, producing the same glorious expression he wore when I had just given birth. He beamed in the presence of creation!

Elizabeth Barrett Browning, Eat Your Heart Out

How do I love you?
I don't know.
 I can't answer that so quickly.
Are you reading Elizabeth's poem to Bob?
Remember, Dear:
 She was sickly.
She only could sit
On her lounge and emit
 Phrases lofty and sweet
To fortunate Browning,
Without any clowning
 He worshiped all day at her feet.
She ranted of heights,
And raved about depths,
 Which his love had inspired.
I'd sure love to do
The same thing for you,
 But, really, I'm terribly tired.
My depth is depression;
My height is the stairs,
 Which I seem to be endlessly climbing,
And why ask me now
When I'm scrubbing the floor?
 Where is *your* fine sense of timing?
Although this falls short
Of romantic retort,
 Which men seem to find so attractive,

How Do I Love You

My love isn't *less*
Than the love she professed,
    It's just that my love is more active!

"I really must work on a paper for my World Lit course," I said as I walked downstairs to answer John and Peter's signal that nap-time was over. "Maybe I'll get a chance to begin it tonight."

At nearly one and two years old, their signal took the form of giggles and exchanges of baby communication between the two little soul mates.

"Why did you start back to college with five courses?" Bernard asked as he followed me downstairs.

"For a couple of reasons. First, I want to finish the three years I need in as close to three years as possible. Besides, taking one course or two at a time would be boring and never ending."

"Therese, I don't know if you're aware of it or not, but there's been a hole in the right pocket of my cashmere overcoat for quite a while now," Bernard announced as we each lifted a smiling son fresh from sleep.

"You're joking, aren't you?" I smiled.

"No. I'm serious. There *is* a hole in the right pocket. When do you think you'll be able to mend that?" he asked seriously.

"Let's see. How about August of '68? I hope to be an alum by then," I chuckled. "By the way, should I expect the usual trip to Europe as a graduation gift?"

"Well if you could show me how to use the sewing machine I could do it myself," he suggested, feeling like low man on the totem pole.

"I'll get to it. I promise. Just remind me next time I have the machine set up. Never mind. I'll do it now by hand before the troops arrive from school. It'll only take a minute."

As surely as the little boys needed a diaper change, the tall boy needed to be reassured that he also counted. Easily managed. Two minutes with needle and thread and all was well.

Three of my favorite men smiled a welcome as I entered the living room. No more needs to be met — for at least a few minutes when the scholars would return home!

"Would you like to go to Europe when you graduate?" he asked, now that his mind had been cleared of the overwhelming burden of a quarter-size hole in the gray velvet pocket of his navy blue overcoat. "Would you prefer to fly or sail?"

"Surprise me!" I answered, as the sound of the school bus brakes announced the arrival of the remaining characters in the drama called, "Life on Swan Street."

Alps

"I can't get over these mountains. Breathtaking!" I gasped.

"Very punny! You can't get over the mountains! I don't believe you!" Anne responded.

"Tell me we don't have to go anywhere near them! What do you see on the map, Anne?" I asked.

"Nothing to worry about, Mom. No elevation on the map for the route we're taking. Probably only have to travel foothills," my navigator consoled.

"Great! You know me. I'm as high as I care to be, sitting in this bus. Crossing mountains is out of the question. Wouldn't add a thing to my personality," I said, relieved.

"Why are you afraid of being up high, Mommy?" Peter asked.

"I don't know, Peter. I wish I weren't but … ," I started.

"But, you just are!" he concluded.

"Sorry, but yes. I just am," I said. "But we don't have to think about that now. We're staying close to the valley. Let's sing!"

"Oh the van went over the mountain,

The van went over the mountain,

The van went over the mountain,"

Several of the older passengers sang.

"That's not funny," I squirmed. "Sing something happy."

"And that is the way we all died!" one joker added.

"Oh, that's pleasant!" I commented, still smiling in the knowledge that altitude wasn't in our immediate future.

"Looks like we're climbing a little bit, Anne. Are you sure we won't be higher than foothills?" I asked.

"I'm certain," said Anne assuredly. "Look at the map!"

"I trust you. It's just that we are climbing. What does that sign say? Never mind, I can read it. It says, '4 *lacets*.' I wonder what that means? *Lacet*? Hmm."

"I don't know," the navigator answered, a little less sure this time.

"Egad! What a miserable turn! It would be bad enough in a car but in this bus it's almost impossible. Oh! Here comes another one and not a damn guardrail in sight. This is crazy! Another hairpin turn. Oh, God! Great foothills!" I moaned.

"I guess *lacets* means hairpin turns," someone from the rear of the bus suggested.

"Oh, no! Eight lacets coming up!" Joseph stage-whispered.

"Don't tell Mommy!" Ed recommended.

"Oh — O-oh no, I can't do this!" I moaned.

"It's all wight Mommy. Don't cwy," John said, using his most soothing tone.

"It's not all right at all. We shouldn't be here. Everyone sit on the floor! Get in the middle! Everyone, now! Don't say anything!" I ordered.

"Ten thousand, four hundred and fifty feet that last sign said," Chris confided to her fellow floor-sitters. "That's about two miles. We're about two miles up in the air right now."

"O-o-oh," I moaned. Crying was out. Tears would blur my vision. Moaning was my only acceptable outlet.

"Mommy, my legs are cramped. Could I sit up on the seat for a minute? I promise I'll be very quiet and I'll sit very still. I promise," Liz pleaded.

"Okay, okay. Sit absolutely still. One at a time, everyone get up very carefully. Don't look out! O-o-oh ... ," I whimpered.

"There are twenty-three cars behind us," Ed announced.

"Twenty-four!" Mary corrected. "It's 'cause we're going so slow."

"Slowly! Not slow!" I instructed, still the teacher at ten thousand feet. Then I wondered why I had corrected her. We're all about to die, anyway. Why do we have to be grammatically correct?

"O-o-h God help me! Can you imagine that stupid man passing us and taking a hand off the wheel to gesture like that?" I commented.

"Maybe he's not scared. Look how fast he's going. He's turning around to shake his fist at us. Why is he doing that, Mommy?" Thérèse asked.

"Because he's crazy! That's why. And rude besides," I answered.

"And French!" added Anne.

"Whee, there goes another car past us. German license plate. He's screaming something at us. He's mad," observed Chris.

"Stark, raving," I added. "Cover your ears. Never mind. They're all swearing in foreign tongues. You wouldn't understand anyway. The gestures *alone* are universal."

"I wonder why there's a white cross on the side of the road?" Peter pondered.

"Shhh," Joseph whispered. "It means a car went over the side at that point."

"O-o-h, please be quiet," I begged.

"Eight *lacets*, but now we're going down," Anne encouraged.

"I think it's worse going down! You can see too much. Don't look! Oh, God. I just hit a boulder. Everybody sit still until I get the wheel over the large rock. Slow … slow … there … now we're off the rock," I announced.

"Are you getting used to the mountain now, Mommy?" Liz asked.

"Now that we're almost finished with the mountain, I'm all right," I lied.

"Where are we now?" Ed asked.

"In the most beautiful valley I've ever seen!" I said. "Thank God, we're finally on flat land. That was awful. I hope I never have to do a thing like that again as long as I live. I'm exhausted. My hands hurt from holding the wheel so tightly."

"Why don't you pull off the road and rest awhile?" Anne suggested. "I'm really sorry. I didn't think we had to cross a mountain."

"That's all right. I'm okay now. That was brutal. So, where are we now, Anne?" I asked.

"I'm not sure where we are. We'll end up in Nice so I guess we, well, this is the only road, so Nice must be straight ahead."

"You know at a time like this I envy men. If I were a man, I'd head for the nearest bar, slam down a shot of whatever and head back to the bus, renewed or at least refueled," I complained.

"Well there's no bar in sight and besides you don't drink. What else could you do?" Anne asked.

"Nothing. I was simply ranting. I'm fine as long as the mountain is behind us," I assured her.

"Are we almost there, Mommy, wherever we're going?" asked Thérèse.

"I hope so, dear, and when we get to Nice, we'll swim in the warm ocean and play in the cool sand, okay?" I smiled weakly.

For a while we drove happily along, laughter and relaxation replaced the moaning and white knuckles that alpine travel had produced.

"Mommy, I don't want to upset you, but I think we're climbing again. Yes we are and there is another sign, you know telling about hairpin turns," Liz offered.

"Another mountain? Oh, God! Haven't these people ever heard of tunnels?" I demanded to know.

"Mommy's praying again," Peter whispered to Liz.

"Yes, she is," Liz agreed.

"She prays at the top of the mountain and at the bottom," Peter advised.

"No, Peter. That's not true," Liz answered.

"Yes. Listen," he said.

"She prays at the top of the mountain and moans. Then at the bottom, she cries and curses," Liz pointed out.

"She says God a lot, I know," Peter noticed.

"Yes, but listen! At the bottom, she adds another word that begins with D, and then 'mountains'," Liz concluded.

Some things are learned too late in life to be of much use. I discovered that while shopping in a supermarket or department store, the natives would scatter in all directions the minute I started to sing along with piped-in music. They left even faster if I threatened to dance a little. All those years of shopping could have been quiet, solo pursuits had I only known. Similarly I learned there *was* a tunnel through the Maritime Alps. Who knew?

Finally in Nice, we sought lodging with no success. Exhausted from unintentional alpine travel, I desperately needed a soft, welcoming bed in which to relax and forget the recent past.

While Joseph was inside the hotel attempting to secure lodging for ten, my hands uncurled and white knuckles disappeared.

Joseph returned with bad news and not-so-bad news. There were no hotel rooms available in the entire area. The not-so-bad news was a suggestion from the night clerk that we park in the courtyard, beneath a large tree where we could safely sleep in the van. There went any thoughts of room service.

Early morning brought a group of curious hotel employees who surrounded the van and counted bodies ... sleeping bodies. My slightly open right eyelid did not qualify me as awake. Soon the sleepy heads stretched, yawned and sat up. We smoothed our clothes as well as possible and slunk into the hotel restrooms. We brushed teeth and hair, washed hands and faces then proudly ordered breakfast.

There we were in outfits we had donned twenty-four hours previously not noticeably different from others. Yes, there we were, slightly wrinkled enjoying crepes, fruit and café au lait on the French Riviera. Gentle, warm sea breezes welcomed us as they wafted across the terrace. We giggled at the thought of what we had just pulled off. Liz wondered if anyone had noticed our less-than-chic attire. I assured her that sweet smiles on the children's faces had kept eyes off the wrinkled wrapping. The truth is, most people don't truly care about how anyone looks except themselves.

At last, our day at the beach became a reality at Nice.

Our senses were bombarded: cool sand between toes; salty, caressing breezes; happy white clouds against azure sky, meeting aquamarine water with gentle surf. This had to be the place where someone clever had coined the expression "Ooh-la-la!"

The kids swam, floated, laughed and reveled in the pleasure of the moment. I opted for the spirit-lifting JOY that came in the form of eight beautiful letters:

S-E-A L-E-V-E-L!

Diagnosis

During the five years he was an invalid, Bernard complained very little.

On those rare occasions when he wondered aloud why this had happened to him at such a young age, I explained it was a gift from God to have these years in which to enjoy the fruits of his labor. Having worked six days a week with little time home, he hardly knew us and how we lived, how we appreciated the lovely home that he had built for us, how close the children were and how much love lived in our home.

Several friends had confessed to me that when they were feeling depressed they would visit us and leave on top of the world, life in perspective once again. My response was always the same: "Sure you feel better, refreshed, because you can drive away from all this and be thankful you don't have to deal with the madness!"

I joked when I said that.

I watched as each visitor was absorbed into the family, enveloped by the pure love of children. No self-serving motive. No hidden agenda. A simple, generous outpouring of the best gift life can bestow: unconditional love. A poet said, it is no small thing when one of these, so fresh from the hand of God, loves us.

Love is palpable. Love heals, if we let it.

Two or three weeks before Bernard died, he told me that he had started to spit up blood. I assumed the blood came in minuscule amounts, but he estimated closer to a quarter of a cup. It had happened several times, he said. He was very weak as he sank into the sofa. I headed for the phone. He said he'd call the doctor as soon as he felt stronger. Not a good time for an argument. He was too weak to stand.

Wasn't it yesterday when my strong, young husband took six stairs in two strides with those long legs? He, my strength, had slowly crumbled and my rebellious spirit refused to accept with resignation the inevitable.

"Let me call while you rest," I offered. "Which doctor? You've told me as much as I need to know. If he has any questions, I'll ask you."

"I need to shave before I leave the house, but I can't right now," he said.

I offered to do the job, knowing full well what his answer would be. Bernard letting me shave him would be comparable to Vince Lombardi allowing his wife to coach the Green Bay Packers because he had a head cold. But he surprised me, letting me shave him, neck and all.

When he finally felt strong enough, he called the doctor. I listened as he explained what was happening, just as he had explained it to me. It was painful to hear his weakened voice estimate how much blood he was losing.

I was thrilled that he had agreed to call for help, which was not easy for him to do, and was sure at least an office visit but more likely hospitalization was to come. I loved taking care of him, but this was out of my league. Thank God, he called the doctor.

But which doctor had he called? The dunce — the *soundman* — who, rather than seek to cure my husband's ills, wanted instead to record five distinct sounds made by Bernard's heart, the one who had misdiagnosed his condition in the first place.

Now he dared to tell Bernard he wasn't losing that amount of blood, that it was simply capillaries bursting that caused bits of blood to appear when he coughed. He didn't want to see him; it was not necessary.

I don't know why I didn't take the phone and tell that medical clod a thing or two. Had I chosen that path, I would have exacerbated an already tense situation. I had to let Bernard be in charge of when to call the doctor and which doctor to call. This was important to him who at the time was not in any condition to be in charge of much else.

"Grit your teeth and keep quiet!" I demanded of myself.

Looking back, I can think, "What if I had insisted about this? What if I had questioned that?" A pointless exercise.

In that day and age, deference was rampant: toward members of the clergy, medical doctors and educators, however lowly. In retrospect, it appears ludicrous.

My attitude toward Bernard was not deferential: Born of love and respect, I cherished his right to be his own man.

As a widow I learned quickly how to confront here or question there when necessary. I became acutely aware that I was one where there should have been two. He whom I had vowed to "love, honor and cherish" was no longer on the scene. Those vows, however, extended to our children. If injustice was suspected, I was up to the task of straightening it out. I learned to fight for me and mine. Alone, I became someone I had never met before. I admired her gutsiness and finally reveled in her "can do" attitude, which could have been hers long before *had she stopped protesting.*

I have often pictured this scenario:

A carefree twenty-four year old was soon to marry her knight in shining armor — Yes!

They would scrimp and save, build a big, beautiful home in a lovely hamlet — Yes!

The lovely home would be filled with many sweet, happy babies — Yes!

DIAGNOSIS

When the knight turned forty-three he would die — No!

At forty-one the once-carefree girl would be a widow — No!

Nine precious lives would be hers alone to guide, protect, teach, nurture, love — No!

"I can't possibly do that, Lord. You've got my shoulders confused with someone else's. If the back is supposed to fit the burden, have you looked at my back lately? I'm not that strong! I know I'm not! I only wanted to be wife and mother. I only wanted to love and care for my husband and children and live happily ever after. I wanted to be part of a team. I can't do this alone! *I don't want to!* I don't want it to end like this!"

Thank God the future is hidden from our eyes. Maybe an average twenty-four year old could have viewed that future and accepted it in stride. I was *never* average, always a dreamer of dreams. I sort of floated through life, thrilled at a clear blue sky, renewed every October by the magnificent foliage, the fragrance of McIntosh apples, walks through dried leaves, crisp fall days with the gift of rosy cheeks. I was carried away by poetry and song: hopeless when either was delivered in a deep, rich voice. Dancing? Most important. Well maybe second after looking good.

I was twenty-four going on ten.

¡Ole!

(H)¡OLE! IN ONE!

"Look! There's an ad for bull-fights on the side of that bus," Ed noticed.

"Have you ever been to a bullfight, Mommy?" Peter wanted to know.

"No, honey, never have. There's another ad. Wow! And another. I guess the arena is close by. It's considered an art form and is an important part of Spanish culture," I added.

¡OLE!

"Mommy?" Peter asked. "Are there any lady bullfighters?"

"I don't know, Peter. I haven't heard of any. There could be. I don't know anything about bullfighting. Uncle Jim told me once that I'd make a good Spanish athlete 'cause I know how to throw the bull. But that's where my knowledge ends," I laughed at the thought.

"Well, maybe there are no lady bullfighters, but I know there *are* lady bulls," Peter declared.

"Now, that's one thing I'm certain of, Peter. A lady bull is called a cow. So there are *no* lady bulls. A bull is male and a cow is female," I corrected him without going into an organ recital.

"Mommy, there *are* lady bulls. I saw it on television. The lady bulls are the ones with the long eyelashes," he assured me. The older kids laughed, and now I'd know a lady bull should I come across one.

"Well, that's good, honey. I'll remember that," I smiled.

"So, are we going to a bullfight?" Joe asked.

"Well, I guess we should," I answered less than enthusiastically, not wanting to inflict my chicken attitude upon the group.

"They advertised them in Spain and we didn't go. Probably won't go here in Majorca, either," Mary observed.

"We'll go to a bullfight if you'd like. Everybody want to go?" I was hoping for a holdout or two. No such luck.

"Yeah!" came the chorus.

"On the way back to the hotel, could we pick up a souvenir each?" asked Ed.

"Sure. This is our last stop — Majorca. Remember to buy something made here. No sense in buying something in Majorca ... ," I started.

"That was made in Japan!" they all chorused and lost control in gales of laughter.

"All right, wise guys. That's enough," I said.

"Look, Mommy, a wig shop. Nothing but wigs. Why don't you try some on?" Mary suggested.

"Why?" I asked, "Does my hair look that bad? Don't answer that. The Parisian coif lasted about twelve hours. Until it grows out, I'm stuck with this. Maybe a wig is a good idea."

Inside the shop, everyone tried on wigs. When the girls tired of seeing themselves in wigs, they tried them on Peter and John. The clerks watched in amazement as the routine played out in orderly fashion. Chris was a redhead, then a short-haired brunette, switch with Mary, then Mary tried on a long blonde number, handed it off to Chris.

At last, I found the wig I'd only dreamed about: shoulder length, a shade lighter than auburn of heavy Spanish hair. It was love at first sight. I bought it. It became part of me. We left the shop, remaining wigs back on their original stands. Everything very much the same as when we arrived, except me. I had a whole new look and was ready for anything, even a bullfight.

Back at the hotel, we freshened up for lunch and would later substitute a round of "Ole's" for a siesta.

Enter the souvenir hunters wearing sombreros forty-eight inches wide.

"Aren't these great?" Joe asked.

"And they were only three dollars each!" Ed added.

Reading my face, Joe quickly added, "And they were made *here*!"

"That's good. Mind telling me how we're going to carry them home? You know we're leaving in a few days. They surely won't fit in a suitcase," I said, raining on their parade.

"But, Mom, you said we should buy something that was made here," Joe explained.

"I know," I mumbled.

"And they didn't really cost that much," Ed chimed in.

"Right," I conceded.

"Well, let's have lunch and check a bus schedule for our trip to the arena," I said.

Entering the dining room, we were, as usual, greeted by a fellow American, his wife (who only smiled) and their 2-point-0 children. The father spoke the same words to his children at every meal: "See all the kids, kids? Look at all the kids!"

How dull can you get? As God made them, He matched them. Every lunch and every dinner, when offered a cornucopia of desserts, she always replied, "Grapesss, pleassse."

After the first two times, this had become deliciously predictable to our family who, with pursed lips, would mouth the words with her, just low enough to be inaudible to all but our table. Of course, this was followed by paralyzing laughter and an inability to finish eating or even order dessert. Just about the time the laughter stopped, the father would comment, "See all the laughing kids, kids?" This was the cue to start the laughter all over again.

A quick trip to our rooms for cameras and a last-minute bathroom check brought us to the bus in plenty of time. The bus ride was short and uneventful, except for a sighting of the Typical American Family a few blocks from the hotel. "See all the kids, kids?" and "Grapesss, pleassse" filled the bus. Waves were exchanged as we passed the foursome.

We chose seats casually, having entered a nearly empty stadium. We saw signs that designated one side as sunny, but what difference would that make? We found out soon enough that a blinding sun made viewing difficult on the side we had chosen.

"Good we have these big hats, Mom, isn't it?" Ed asked.

"Sure is. Good for you and three people on either side of you. All that shade for three dollars," I agreed, with just a touch of sarcasm. The arena filled up rapidly. Bullfight devotees came well-equipped with cushions, a taste of the bubbly and sunshields.

There we sat, squinting and hoping for the best. Suddenly, I felt a touch claustrophobic. I wondered out loud how one or ten would possibly leave in an emergency. The place was filled beyond capacity, jam-packed.

The first man-versus-beast contest was announced. The announcement in Spanish temporarily distracted me from maternal, protective thoughts. I relaxed and was ready to be educated in this "cultural experience." Why not be a child with the children and simply enjoy? I did just that. For a good thirty seconds. Then those dreaded words came out of an angel's mouth. Looking up at me with his Daddy's hazel eyes, John confided, "I have to go to the bathroom. Now!"

"Oh God!" were my exact words.

"Edward, pass me your sombrero, please," I quietly said as I leaned forward and looked past three of the children who separated Ed's seat from mine.

"You want my sombrero? You're kidding, right?" he asked.

"But I thought you were mad that we bought them," he said, puzzled.

"No, I'm serious. Please pass it down," I pleaded.

"You really want my sombrero!" he said.

"Give me the *damn* hat!" I snarled through clenched teeth. The hat came my way. "Okay, John, stand in front of me, and Joe, hand me your empty soda bottle."

The flexible sombrero had shielded John on three sides, I made up the fourth side for John who held the soda bottle and hit a hole in one with complete privacy in the overcrowded stadium. From that time on, hitting the bottle has had a whole new connotation for me. Our shouts of "Ole!" left other fans wondering, since action on the floor hadn't begun. The bullfights paled in comparison to what I considered the main event that afternoon.

¡OLE!

I've read about bullfighting and watched with the hope that I would gain insight into what constitutes the charm of this event, but it eluded me. Where is the sport or art in sticking a poor, dumb animal with picks to drive it mad before it dies? One matador, the bull felled, bent to kiss his victim on the nose. Suddenly the human was airborne, cape flapping in the breeze. He landed with a thud. Was I alone in wanting to scream "Ole" *for the bull*? So much for cultural experiences!

Flood

"Mrs. Kramer, you have a telephone call. You can take it in the office," called the secretary at St. Thomas Aquinas College, as I sat making a wall plaque out of clay, which ironically read, "This too will pass."

On the walk to the office I tried to imagine why anyone would call me at school. This was the busy last semester, which included student teaching and two last courses required for graduation.

My hello was answered by Edward, then 11, calling from home.

"Edward, this better be good," I bristled. "Why are you calling me at school?"

"I'm sorry, Mom, but I didn't know what else to do," he apologized. "Water is coming out of the dishwasher, a lot of water!"

"Are you in the kitchen now?" I asked.

"No, the water's too deep in there."

"I'm on my way," I said. "I'll be right there."

Water coming from the dishwasher, how bad could that be? It sprays water and then there's some sitting in the bottom of the machine when the cycle is interrupted. Maybe ten gallons tops. Probably not that bad.

Pollyanna exited when I entered the house through the garage. Water greeted me in the laundry room, more as I sloshed through the kitchen into the dining room, which was only partially flooded. Water seeped through the oak floors into the finished basement, ruining the ceiling in the bargain. Still the water poured out of the dishwasher. There was nothing to do but let it, no valve to shut.

"Hurry, bring all the newspapers from the living room!" I ordered.

"We used them already, Mom, before Edward called you," Mary said.

"All right, get all the towels, bedspreads, get ... oh damn it! Empty both linen closets ... hurry! Drop everything in the water, wring it out outside. Keep doing that until all the water is gone," I ordered as I watched water continue to pour out of the dishwasher.

Once, six months or so before he died, Bernard had shown me a valve in the basement.

"This is where you turn the water off," he instructed. "Just turn it clockwise and no water comes into the house."

I listened but told him that was his department. The valve prevented inflow of water intended for the house. This was a freak thing. This was not supposed to be happening. Several hours later the water stopped, every piece of linen we owned was draped over the patio walls to dry somewhat before laundering. The washer and dryer ran non-stop until midnight, nearly completing the job.

Somewhere shortly after dark, I drove to the store, bought a pack of cigarettes and started a habit that I had forsaken more than thirteen years before. I sat at the kitchen table crying in desperation, puffing on cigarettes soggy with tears.

My act of frustration inspired others to act out in lively scenarios.

Joseph asked, "Why are you doing this? Don't you remember you gave up smoking when I was born? Why are you doing this? Don't you care what happens to me?" assuming if I had given up smoking in thanksgiving for his birth, resuming smoking could reverse the procedure.

This was followed by a parade of children from the bar in the living room to the trash can in the kitchen where the contents of the bar were deposited. Beefeaters, Dewars, Canadian Club became one at the bottom of the trashcan.

"What's the matter with you?" I cried. "What are you doing?"

"We decided that if you started smoking again, next you'd start drinking, so we're getting rid of the liquor," Mary explained.

"That's ridiculous!" I protested. "When have you ever seen me drink except when we have guests?"

"Yeah, but we never saw you smoke before either," Edward finished the discussion.

"Well, we've had hell and high water. What next?" I wept and wondered alone at the kitchen table between loads of laundry.

Accustomed to being part of a team, I felt myself rebelling at what I called "being in charge," a misnomer for being alone. I had always been "in charge" — raising the children, doctor and dentists' appointments, PTA meetings, purchases for the home and family, paying bills, home and yard maintenance. I managed them all happily while Bernard worked six days a week. On Sunday, he was free to relax, but most Sunday evenings found him pacing, anxious to return to his world of work.

Alone after Bernard's death, I exaggerated the need for me to do both jobs. I looked over the house carefully, trying to look at things as a man would. Everything looked pretty good. Why not? It was a gorgeous, well-constructed ten-year-old house. What could go wrong?

Let's see. The wooden gutters will rot in time. I decided I would have them replaced with aluminum gutters. Having made this unnecessary but definite decision, I contacted a New York City cop moonlighting as a handyman. I explained what I wanted done and together we decided a dry well in the backyard was also a good idea. Work was done well and on time. While we walked around

184

the house, I was satisfied with the new look, adding one request, that the elbow at the bottom of the downspout be turned outward toward the driveway. No problem, he assured me. I went inside for his check, assuming he was busy turning the elbow.

I folded the last load of wash for the night. I turned on the outside spotlight to check the direction of the elbow. It was turned *inward* toward the front yard. The January thaw had emptied snow from the roof into the massive dry well, which ordinarily caught only kitchen and laundry room water. Snow from the roof had previously traveled down the side of the driveway with the elbow turned correctly in that direction.

At least now I knew the reason behind the flood. I fell into bed about one a.m., exhausted. Later I'd contact the insurance company to find out the damage wasn't covered because it came from the outside of the house. For now, I needed to sleep, to face in a few hours the usual morning routine: getting the school kids on their way, dropping Peter and John at nursery school and heading to Monsey, New York, for a pleasant day of student teaching.

Shakespeare saved the day with his bolstering, "All the world's a stage."

In a matter of hours, the stage would be mine again.

Homeward Bound

"Everyone check closets, dressers, desks, under beds and everywhere to be sure we're not forgetting anything!" I announced.

"Are we leaving before dinner?" Liz asked.

"No, we're leaving late tonight, but it wouldn't hurt to get a head start on emptying drawers and closets. We'll pack everything except a complete change of clothes for everyone. When that's done, we'll go to the beach for a few hours, relax, come back to the hotel, shower, dress, have dinner and then it'll be time to leave for the boat to Barcelona," I answered.

"Isn't it a ship that we take to Barcelona? You called it a boat," Mary wanted to know.

"I don't know when a sea-going vessel is called a boat or a ship. It's probably something technical, like how many knots an hour it travels, the size of the engines or something like that," I replied.

"So then if you don't know the answer, why'd you call it a boat?" Edward joined in.

"I think that something that carries passengers between a country and an island and vice versa should be called a ferry, boat or ferryboat, but if it's sailing way out on the ocean it should be called a ship," I explained.

"Remember when you and Daddy went on a Caribbean cruise?" Mary continued.

"Ah, yes, I remember it well," I sang.

"Well that sailed from New York to several islands but you called that a cruise ship. So why do you call what we're taking tonight a boat?" Mary asked.

"'Cause boat sounds better with Barcelona!" I said, ending the nautical inquisition. "Have you finished packing?"

Back from the beach, sandy, rosy and refreshed, we showered, some napped, some checked to be certain important souvenirs were safely packed and all dressed leisurely for our last dinner in Mallorca.

"Mommy, tomorrow we'll be home!" Liz smiled.

187

"Yes, honey. God willing," I answered.

"Why do you always say that?" Chris asked. "Why wouldn't He be willing? We have to go to school next week."

"I'm sure He's willing us a safe trip home. I say 'God willing' as a way of saying God is in charge. We aren't. We can make plans but sometimes the Lord has something else in mind for us."

"You mean like when Daddy died?" she wondered, "because you didn't plan that?"

"That's right. Like that. Remember the poem that talks about London being a man's town and Paris as a woman's town?" I said, changing the subject.

"I remember," several voices responded, "Why? We're not going back, are we?" they mumbled.

"No, we're not going back. But I've saved the best part of the poem until now."

"What is the best part?" Liz asked.

"Tis fine to see the Old World,
And travel up and down
Among the famous palaces
And cities of renown,
To admire the crumbly castles
And the statues of the kings,
But now I think I've had enough
Of antiquated things.
So it's home again, and home again,
America for me!
My heart is turning home again,
And there I long to be
In the land of youth and freedom
Beyond the ocean bars,
Where the air is full of sunlight
And the flag is full of stars."

188

Once on board the sea-going vessel, I asked a crewman whether he expected rough seas. Of course this was done with body language: For rough seas, one points to the ship, extends her hands, leaving about a foot of space between them, and gently rocks the hands, maintaining a quizzical facial expression. On the cruise from Barcelona I had asked the same question and the answer was an emphatic, "Pacifico!" I'd hate to experience "turbulento" or however you say "rough" in Spanish if he had told the truth about calm seas in the one-word assurance, "Pacifico."

I spent that entire eight-hour voyage between Majorca and Barcelona running between state rooms, securing the children in their bunks; rolled blankets became buffers between a child and the hard floor below. Back in my stateroom on that "Pacifico" crossing, secure that everyone was safe, I tried to sleep, but each roll of the ship sent me off again to check on my babes.

I hoped this crossing to Spain would be calm and sleep-filled. It was.

From the ship to the airport, a flight from Barcelona to Lisbon, an hour layover and then we were truly homeward bound. If I recall correctly, the flight was nine hours, including the short flight to Portugal and the hour delay.

Some of the passengers on the homebound flight whiled away the long hours with a glass of the bubbly followed by many more of the same. Party hearty was the rule of the flight.

Directly in front of us sat an attractive gentleman who, after he'd had a few, invited all ten of us to visit him for an extended stay at his home in California. I assumed, as my mother would have said, "it was the drink talking" and graciously declined.

Sleep for the kids was out of the question: Anticipation of home had dropped a cloud of cordiality over the entire group.

Smiles abounded, some played cards, others chatted and they all reminisced like retired people.

Our landing at Kennedy Airport was accompanied by much applause by the cheer-filled passengers. We left the plane together and headed toward luggage retrieval.

Peter, whose hand I held, shouted, "Hurry, Mommy. Look! Our flag!"

I shared his enthusiasm and marveled at his beautiful awareness of home — not simply as our house in Palisades but the grander notion of our great country as Home, with a capital H.

This joy in my boy lasted for at least five minutes until "himself," John and Thérèse hopped aboard the empty luggage carousel. Why not? The mood was festive, we were home and an empty carousel called to them.

The customs inspector asked if "all" the luggage and "all" the kids were mine. I smiled and claimed them "all." He said, "Phew," and assured me that his inspection would be brief. I smiled in the direction of the slightly restless natives and said, "Thank you. I'm sure it will be."

A kind friend picked us up at the airport, somehow managing to fit all ten of us, complete with luggage, into a station wagon. I wish I could remember the ride from Kennedy to Palisades, but I can't. I'm sure there was singing. There was always singing in the car. Singing people are less likely to be punching people, I discovered early in the game. I do remember kissing the living room floor when we arrived home, thanking the Lord for a great experience and a safe return.

Luggage remained unpacked until the next day or maybe the day after that. There were more important items on the agenda: a dash to the swim club for a long-awaited dip, meeting friends, chatting merrily about the trip and the prospect of school only a few days off.

The phone rang madly, amid shouts of, "Anyone see my mitt?" and "Mom, is it okay if I sleep over at Sue's tonight?" and "Will I still have a party, 'cause we were away on my birthday?"

Suddenly taking the crew through Europe seemed like a piece of cake in comparison to the madness of being home. Why? It was a strange phenomenon.

I tried to find an explanation while I unpacked, which was simplified by making three stacks: white, light and dark clothes. "Wash it all," I'd decided, remembering Thoreau's, "Simplify. Simplify." The only way to fly!

The house grew abnormally serene. There. That was better. Even the phone had recognized my need for a short period of adjustment. Quiet surrounded me.

I checked the luggage one last time, zipping each bag as I'd finished with it. I discovered quite remarkably that we had arrived home with almost everything with which we'd left.

Not even an odd sock!

I've struggled with the odd-sock question for years. When anyone asked what was most difficult in raising a large family, my answer was, "Odd socks." Now, after nine weeks in Europe, the answer had come to me when I least expected it. The solution to the odd sock puzzle is travel.

Final Note to Parents

So, that's the whole truth concerning our summer abroad. Perhaps reading this madness hasn't dissuaded you from plans to travel, kids in tow.

Fine.

Do it.

However, parent to parent, I want to confide one last *bon mot*: All the kids' belongings were accounted for in the final check. I, however, discovered that I had returned home minus a girdle and one shoe. And, despite the loss of such personal items, I didn't have *that* much fun!

A Postscript To My Children

"How did you manage?"

"Did you cry all day?"

"Did you wish you didn't have children so you could be free?"

"How did you know what to do?"

"Were you really brave and strong?"

"Did you talk to him even though he wasn't here?"

"When you had a house full of teenagers did you feel like screaming?"

"If you had known you'd be a widow at forty-one, would you have married?"

"Was it lonely for you with only kids and work?"

These are some of the many questions you have asked since those days.

I'll answer them as honestly as I can.

I managed by going through the motions of our everyday lives, doing mundane chores, laundry, shopping, cooking. Take note: I didn't mention dusting; I said I'd answer *honestly*.

No, I didn't cry all day. I couldn't afford that luxury. The long nights, however, were mine alone.

I *never* wished you weren't in my life; I wanted each and every one of you. You were and *are* my life; my greatest blessings, warts and all.

How did I know what to do?

I didn't.

There are no dress rehearsals for widowhood. I truly wish it were otherwise, but no, I was not brave and strong. Deep inside me I kicked, screamed, ranted and raved emotionally, stating in no uncertain terms that widowhood was not what I had signed up for. I wanted to be part of a team: one is a horrible number.

Paradoxically, I knew I *could* do it but I fought against having the terms of the contract changed without my consent.

Strange as it may seem, I had felt totally free-spirited, joyous as the mother of a large family, caring for an invalid husband and finishing college. Why not be joyous? I was doing all the things I wanted to do!

I reacted like a spoiled child. Widowhood burdened me. It had not been my choice. It was inflicted upon me. I argued with the Coach! The Coach smiled very slightly as He watched me rebel knowing that the fierce fight I put up came from a vibrant spirit that would be the very thing I needed to do the job as soon as the dust cleared and I could see again.

Yes, I often spoke to Daddy, even though he wasn't there. Someone wisely observed that death ends a life, but not a relationship. So true.

Me, scream, simply because the house was filled with teenagers? Screaming has never been a habit of mine so I didn't scream, I didn't drink, either, though an occasional sense-numbing libation might well have helped me feel less of the madness which is adolescence.

I often wondered about my generation as teenagers. Were we innocent or ignorant? What was the difference between our kids and us? Our high school years were war years. Negative feelings were easily directed toward "enemies" who had started the war in Europe and the Pacific. Our parents were not the enemies. How come you guys didn't know that?

Had the future been shown to me would I have married, had you all, knowing that at forty-one the job would be mine alone to do? This is tricky. I shouldn't confess this, but it is true. Twenty-four was my chronological age when I married, but my mental age hovered closer to eighteen. Please don't be disappointed by this disclosure; I cared a *lot* about how I dressed and looked and how a date danced. Superficial? I'm sure. Good dancer with a great sense of humor? Oh, yeah!

So, you can guess the answer to would I have signed up for life as it played out? Never! Why would a frivolous dreamer do such a thing? I am *thrilled* no such preview was mine to view. I'd have refused the offer and, in the adamant refusal, would have missed *life*.

Was it lonely with only kids and work?

Only after 1973, when a persistent health problem began.

The same spirit, however, which had me rebel against widowhood, and dared me to survive your teen years is still hanging in there. Maybe I've evolved from a frivolous young adult to a tough old dame who still feels like eighteen — until she looks in the mirror!

I've told you too much already. No more questions! I hope you enjoy this memoir covering roughly seven years of a fabulous life. Thanks for your great company in those years that, in retrospect, were a mere handful of minutes. And thank you for all that great material, much of which makes this book. (Lord knows, there was enough material to fill several large volumes, but since discretion is the better part of valor, I opted to fill only these few pages.)

I love, love, love you all collectively and individually. Being your mother has been and continues to be my greatest privilege.

T.P.K.